# CAREGIVER'S
# DEVOTIONAL
## *Serving Others in Love*

KAY TUEL

2021

PROFESSIONAL PUBLISHING MEETS POWERFUL PROMOTION

A wholly owned subsidiary of TBN

Trilogy Christian Publishers
A Wholly Owned Subsidiary of Trinity Broadcasting Network
2442 Michelle Drive
Tustin, CA 92780

Scripture quotations marked (NIV) taken from *Life Application Study Bible: New International Version*. 2012. Wheaton, Ill: Tyndale House Publishers, Inc.

Scripture quotations marked (*MSG*) taken from Petterson, Eugene H. 2005. *The Message*. Tyndale House Publishers, Inc. https://www.biblegateway.com/versions/Message-MSG-Bible/#booklist.

Scripture quotations marked (ASV) taken from *The Holy Bible: American Standard Version*. 1901. Thomas Nelson and Sons. Public domain. https://www.biblegateway.com/versions/American-Standard-Version-ASV-Bible/#booklist.

Scripture quotations marked (AMP) taken from *The Holy Bible: Amplified Bible*. 2015. La Habra, California: The Lockman Foundation. https://www.biblegateway.com/versions/Amplified-Bible-AMP/#booklist.

Scripture quotations marked (BSB) taken from *The Holy Bible: Berean Study Bible*. 2016. 1st editio. https://biblehub.com/bsb/genesis/1.htm.

Scripture quotations marked (ESV) taken from *The Holy Bible: English Standard Version*. 2007. Wheaton, Ill: Crossway Bibles. Public domain. https://www.biblegateway.com/versions/English-Standard-Version-ESV-Bible/#booklist.

Scripture quotations marked (NASB) taken from *The Holy Bible: New American Standard Bible*. 2015. The Lockman Foundation. http://www.lockman.org/nasb/index.php.

Scripture quotations marked (NASB 1995*MSG*) taken from *The Holy Bible: New American Standard Bible*. 1995. The Lockman Foundation. http://www.lockman.org/nasb/index.php.

Scripture quotations marked (NLT) taken from *The Holy Bible: New Living Translation*. 2013. Carol Stream: Tyndale House Foundation. Tyndale House Publishers, Inc. https://www.biblegateway.com/versions/New-Living-Translation-NLT-Bible/#booklist.

Scripture quotations marked (TPT) taken from *The Holy Bible: The Passion Translation*. 2020. BroadStreet Publishing Group, LLC.

10 9 8 7 6 5 4 3 2 1
Library of Congress Cataloging-in-Publication Data is available.
ISBN 978-1-63769-786-3

ISBN 978-1-63769-787-0 (eBook)

# DEDICATION

This book is dedicated to my mother and father, who lived this journey with me and taught me the life lessons of caregiving. I also inscribe this to my grandchildren Norah, Beau, Cleet, and Sloane, so they will be reminded that a key focus of their heritage is to demonstrate the love of Christ by serving others.

# TABLE OF CONTENTS

# INTRODUCTION

At the time of this writing, I have cared for my father for over eighteen years and my mother for eight years. There are different seasons of caregiving, and after several years I found it was therapeutic to journal. The Lord met me as I wrote, and these devotionals are an outcome of years of walking this journey.

My hope is that the writings will encourage those who are on this expedition. It is my desire that readers know they are not alone and others have survived and grown deeper in intimacy with Christ as they have walked through the different seasons of caregiving. I pray the Lord will meet you as you read.

# HE KNOWS

God's name is "El Deah". The God who knows every-thing. Everything. He knows everything that is going to happen, and none of it ever takes Him by surprise. Our God sees the beginning, the middle, and the end... all at once, all the time. No surprises.

This means He knows our situation. He is not surprised. He knows how it will end, He knows how it began, and He sees us now right in the middle of it—no surprises to Him.

That's a difficult concept to grasp because we are on a journey that we could not predict. We don't know exactly how it will play out. We have to trust our Heavenly Father because He is El Deah. He knows. We don't know, and we have to find rest in that.

> Father, teach us to trust you. Teach us to release the orchestration of our future to You. We know you are capable and that You love us. Right now, as much as we are able, we lay our burdens at Your feet and say, take them, Father. You know the end of the story, so we submit this day and our future to You. Amen.

*The Son is the image of the invisible God, the firstborn over all creation. For in him all things were created: things in heaven and on earth, visible and invisible, whether thrones or powers or rulers or authorities; all things have been created through him and for him. He is before all things, and in him all things hold together.*

**(Colossians 1:15–17 NIV)**

*Trust in him at all times, you people; pour out your hearts to him, for God is our refuge*

**(Psalm 62:8 NIV)**

*You have searched me, L<small>ORD</small>, and you know me. You know when I sit and when I rise; you perceive my thoughts from afar. You discern my going out and my lying down; you are familiar with all my ways. Before a word is on my tongue you, L<small>ORD</small>, know it completely*

**(Psalm 139:1–4 NIV)**

*Great is our Lord and mighty in power; his understanding has no limit.*

**(Psalm 147:5 NIV)**

*Oh, the depth of the riches of the wisdom and knowledge of God! How unsearchable his judgments, and his paths beyond tracing out!*

**(Romans 11:33 NIV)**

# YOU'VE GOT TO LAUGH

This season can be so hard and full of discouraging developments. We have to seek out fun actively! We have to find laughter. It's essential. Seeking joy may also look like purposely not watching movies right now about losing loved ones or about anything with a sad ending. We can search for comedy shows where we can really belly laugh! Also, it's helpful to make time to spend with people who bring us joy. We need other people in this season. I think one reason God equipped us with a sense of humor was to lighten the load of the heavy times. Laughter is a sign of God's joy. If we have nothing else at this moment that we can think of that makes us glad, we can always rejoice in who He is to us.

Thank you, Father, for your gift of laughter. What a clever invention! Lord, you knew we would need joy and delight in this life. You are the originator of joy. You are a creative God. Help me to find humor even in the midst of this season. Amen.

*Rejoice in the Lord always. I will say it again: Rejoice!*

**(Philippians 4:4 NIV)**

*Further, my brothers and sisters, rejoice in the Lord! It is no trouble for me to write the same things to you again, and it is a safeguard for you.*

**(Philippians 3:1 NIV)**

*Rejoice in that day, and leap for joy, for behold, your reward is great in heaven; for so their fathers did to the prophets.*

**(Luke 6:23 ESV)**

*You suffered along with those in prison and joyfully accepted the confiscation of your property, because you knew that you yourselves had better and lasting possessions.*

**(Hebrews 10:34 NIV)**

*Dear friends, do not be surprised at the fiery ordeal that has come on you to test you, as though something strange were happening to you. But rejoice inasmuch as you participate in the sufferings of Christ, so that you may be overjoyed when his glory is revealed.*

**(1 Peter 4:12–13 NIV)**

# NO REGRETS

Let's don't have any regrets; let's face this head-on. Caregiving for a loved one is like bungee jumping with a weak, worn rope. Some weeks their health may be fairly stable, but within a moment, things can change! One fall, fever, or infection can plummet their health. At these times of soaring towards the bottom, we face the question... *Have we said what we want to say to them before they are gone or incapable of knowing us any longer? Is there more we need to say?* Then we realize, none of us know the time or day we will leave this life and enter eternity. *Are there kind words we need to share with someone now? Is there someone who doesn't know about our loving and incredible Jesus yet?* We need to say those things now, to everyone, and not wait.

Dear Father, teach us to be bold and share encouragement with one another. Give us the urgency to say things today to others and to walk in courage without fear or anxiety. Every day from You is a gift! Let us be wise in how we use our days. Let us have sweet moments with our loved one. Amen.

*But encourage one another daily, as long as it is still called "Today," so that none of you may be hardened by sin's deceitfulness.*

**(Hebrews 3:13 NIV)**

*Come now, you who say, "Today or tomorrow we will go into such and such a town and spend a year there and trade and make a profit"—yet you do not know what tomorrow will bring. What is your life? For you are a mist that appears for a little time and then vanishes.*

**(James 4:13–14 ESV)**

*And we urge you, brothers, admonish the idle, encourage the fainthearted, help the weak, be patient with them all.*

**(1 Thessalonians 5:14 ESV)**

*Let the word of Christ dwell in you richly, teaching and admonishing one another in all wisdom, singing psalms and hymns and spiritual songs, with thankfulness in your hearts to God.*

**(Colossians 3:16 ESV)**

*And Judas and Silas, who were themselves prophets, encouraged and strengthened the brothers with many words.*

**(Acts 15:32 ESV)**

# TRYING TO MAKE SOME SENSE OF IT

We don't want to come off as some spiritual superheroes—it is only because of this place of desperation that we genuinely see life is impossible if we try to make sense of it without faith. Being able to find wisdom and encouragement in the Bible during this season is a lifesaver. Crying out to God in anger to release it is an emotional steam valve. We couldn't walk this path well without believing in eternity and hope of more to come than this life. We're no guru or saints, just people who have been stripped of things in life like predictability, order, calm, the health of a loved one, and realized that what is left is actually what is the foundation of life—faith.

Lord, thank you for being our firm foundation. Thank you for being bigger than life here on earth. Thank you for giving us hope beyond this life and beyond our capabilities. We need You. More than that, we want You in our lives. Come and give that peace you promise which is there in spite of circumstances. Amen.

*I keep my eyes always on the Lord. With him at my right hand, I will not be shaken.*

**(Psalm 16:8 NIV)**

*I can do all this through him who gives me strength.*

**(Philippians 4:13 NIV)**

*These words I speak to you are not incidental additions to your life, homeowner improvements to your standard of living. They are foundational words, words to build a life on. If you work these words into your life, you are like a smart carpenter who build his house on solid rock. Rain poured down, the river flooded, a tornado hit—but nothing moved that house. It was fixed to the rock.*

**(Matthew 7:24–27 MSG)**

But if you just use my words in Bible studies and don't work them into your life, you are like a stupid carpenter who built his house on the sandy beach. When a storm rolled in and the waves came up, it collapsed like a house of cards.

*And the peace of God, which transcends all understanding, will guard your hearts and your minds in Christ Jesus.*

**(Philippians 4:7 NIV)**

# JESUS WEPT

We are sad, terribly sad. We're watching our loved one's decline, and we know where we are headed. We'll miss them. We'll yearn for what was. When they are gone, we'll be reminded of them in sounds, smells, pictures, places, and memories. So, it gives us comfort that Jesus wept. It's a normal human emotion to be sad. We're allowed. This season seems to be full of reminders that we are losing them. Sorrow feels as if it is our companion today. But our feelings are natural, not odd. That gives us comfort. Even Jesus cried, so we can too.

Lord, we need you today to give us comfort. We need to be reminded that there will be a reunion in eternity where there will be no sickness or handicaps. Make Your presence tangible to us today. Swaddle us in Your Holy Spirit. Give us the grace to walk through this valley. Amen.

*Out of the depths I cry to you, O Lord; Lord, hear my voice. Let your ears be attentive to my cry for mercy.*

**(Psalm 130:1–2 NIV)**

21

*My soul is weary with sorrow; strengthen me according to your word.*

**(Psalm 119:28 NIV)**

*Jesus wept.*

**(John 11:35 ESV NIV)**

*I waited patiently for the LORD; he turned to me and heard my cry.*

**(Psalm 40:1 NIV)**

*When the righteous cry out for help, the LORD hears and delivers them out of all their troubles.*

**(Psalm 34:17 ESV)**

*The LORD is near to the brokenhearted and saves the crushed in spirit.*

**(Psalm 34:18 ESV)**

# RAISE YOUR GAZE

The Bible instructs us to "Set your minds on things above, not on earthly things" (Colossians 3:2 NIV). God knows the whole story, and this is a golden nugget to survive the struggles of this world: Put our focus on eternity instead of this brief and temporary life. We forget this mindset, and we easily get bogged down in the issues of our days. When we care-give for another, there are so many more issues to contend with that it seems we easily get stuck mentally in the daily tasks at hand. The Lord knew times would be difficult, so He has told us the end of the story to keep us going. We know we have eternity awaiting us! Keep focusing on the finish line and depend on Him to be with you all the way!

Lord, give us Your perspective on our situations. Keep our eyes focused on You as we walk this journey. Remind us of the eternal value in our days and not the present difficulties. You are a good Father! Your plans are good! Eternity will be divine! Please give us reminders of the end goal as we go through our days. Amen.

*Since, then, you have been raised with Christ, set your hearts on things above, where Christ is seated at the right hand of God. Set your minds on things above, not on earthly things. For you died, and your life is now hidden with Christ in God.*

**(Colossians 3:1–3 NIV)**

*he made known to us the mystery of his will according to his good pleasure, which he purposed in Christ, to be put into effect when the times reach their fulfillment—to bring unity to all things in heaven and on earth under Christ.*

**(Ephesians 1:9–10)**

*Therefore, with minds that are alert and fully sober, set your hope on the grace to be brought to you when Jesus Christ is revealed at his coming.*

**(1 Peter 1:13 NIV)**

*For to set the mind on the flesh is death, but to set the mind on the Spirit is life and peace.*

**(Romans 8:6 ESV)**

*You will keep in perfect peace those whose minds are steadfast, because they trust in you.*

**(Isaiah 26:3 NIV)**

*And the peace of God, which transcends all understanding, will guard your hearts and your minds in Christ Jesus.*

**(Philippians 4:7 NIV)**

*But our citizenship is in heaven. And we eagerly await a Savior from there, the Lord Jesus Christ.*

**(Philippians 3:20 NIV)**

*My eyes are ever on the LORD, for only he will release my feet from the snare.*

**(Psalm 25:15 NIV)**

# I AM NOT ALONE

This season in life can be so isolating. Sometimes the only people we see all week are the homecare nurses and caregivers who come. We need others. We wish our friends knew how much a text or email or call encourages us. Maybe people feel that we need quiet? On the contrary, in this difficult part of our journey, we need each other even more! We have to make ourselves call others and write friends. People just don't know what to do, so they do nothing. Let's be the wave of change and teach them how to walk with us. We are not alone!

Father, help us not believe the thoughts that we are alone. Your Holy Spirit is always with us. The Body of Christ is near. Teach us how to reach out for help. Give us the courage to talk to friends even if there is little response. We want to be as one body, going through life seasons together. Bring friends into our lives who will walk this journey with us. Amen.

*And let us consider thoughtfully how we may spur one another on toward love and good deeds, not giving up meeting together, as some are in the habit of doing, but encouraging one another—and all the more as you see the Day approaching.*

**(Hebrews 10:24–25 NIV)**

*Be devoted to one another in love. Honor one another above yourselves. Share with the Lord's people who are in need. Practice hospitality.*

**(Romans 12:10, 13 NIV)**

*For just as each of us has one body with many members, and these members do not all have the same function, so in Christ we, though many, form one body, and each member belongs to all the others.*

**(Romans 12:4–5 NIV)**

*My prayer is not for them alone. I pray also for those who will believe in me through their message, that all of them may be one, Father, just as you are in me and I am in you. May they also be in us so that the world may believe that you have sent me. I have given them the glory that you gave me, that they may be one as we are one—I in them and you in me—so that they may be brought to complete unity. Then the world will know that you sent me and have loved them even as you have loved me.*

**(John 17: 20–23 NIV)**

# WORSHIP ANYWAY

There are days when we don't get anything tangible accomplished. We feel like we are running in circles. We have such good things on our "to do" list. We imagined how productive our day would be... but it wasn't. Frustration can overtake us so easily. We can get annoyed with the situation we are in because our time is unpredictable, and our lists usually don't get completed. Unexpected things are expected every day. So, in the midst of this, even when we don't feel like it, we have to learn to worship.

There is power in what we give to God, especially when He did not come through the way *we* thought He should. God may seem far away, and praise is not natural. To praise Him now requires laying our will down on His altar and choosing to believe that He is good.

Worship causes us to reflect on God instead of our circumstances. Worship brings us closer to Him and can cause us to think more like Him, thus becoming more like Him. We become like those we admire and worship. He is amazingly gracious, merciful, and He is who we want to be like!

Father, remind us to turn to worship even when we feel we're falling behind. Teach us to turn disappointment into praise quickly. Walk with us and whisper where to walk, for there are days we feel we've gotten off the trail and fallen behind. Thank you for Your character, which is encouraging and merciful. Amen.

> But he gives more grace. Therefore it says, "God opposes the proud but gives grace to the humble." Humble yourselves before the Lord, and He will exalt you.
>
> **(James 4:6, 10 ESV)**

> Through Jesus, therefore, let us continually offer to God a sacrifice of praise—the fruit of lips that openly profess his name.
>
> **(Hebrews 13:15 NIV)**

> After they had been severely flogged, they were thrown into prison, and the jailer was commanded to guard them carefully. When he received these orders, he put them in the inner cell and fastened their feet in the stocks. About midnight Paul and Silas were praying and singing hymns to God, and the other prisoners were listening to them..
>
> **(Acts 16:23–25 NIV)**

> Accept, LORD, the willing praise of my mouth, and teach me your laws.
>
> **(Psalm 119:108 NIV)**

*Whether you turn to the right or to the left, your ears will hear a voice behind you, saying, "This is the way, walk in it."*

**(Isaiah 30:21 NIV)**

# RECALCULATING

Seeing our loved one at the end of their journey makes us take inventory of our life. We ask ourselves, *Am I living the life I want to live? Will we look back when we are in their place at the end of our lifespan and say we were content with our choices?* This is a good wake-up call to shift our priorities. Refining reflection helps clarify our choices. We can evaluate our goals again. We can analyze whether our life is honoring Christ if we are deepening our relationship with Him, and if we are loving well. We want to participate in this race. No longer is it a goal to move up the success ladder, collect more degrees, or make a name for ourselves. We want to love Him and love others. We want to head toward the goal God has given us.

Lord, help us head toward your goal. We want to end our life knowing we honored You and, even in the daily mundane things, we want to please You. That's what You look at... our heart in what we do, not that we do magnificent things. Refine our life now, Father, and recalculate our path. Don't let us get caught up in the things of this life that drain us from seeking You. Help us seek You in all our days. Amen.

*I have fought the good fight, I have finished the race, I have kept the faith. Now there is in store for me the crown of righteousness, which the Lord, the righteous Judge, will award to me on that day—and not only to me, but also to all who have longed for his appearing.*

**(2 Timothy 4:7–8 NIV)**

*Not that I have already obtained all this, or have already arrived at my goal, but I press on to take hold of that for which Christ Jesus took hold of me. Brothers and sisters, I do not consider myself yet to have taken hold of it. But one thing I do: Forgetting what is behind and straining toward what is ahead.*

**(Philippians 3:12–13 NIV)**

*Therefore, since we are surrounded by such a great cloud of witnesses, let us throw off everything that hinders and the sin that so easily entangles. And let us run with perseverance the race marked out for us,*

**(Hebrews 12:1 NIV)**

*For no one can lay any foundation other than the one already laid, which is Jesus Christ. If anyone builds on this foundation using gold, silver, costly stones, wood, hay or straw, their work will be shown for what it is, because the Day will bring it to light. It will be revealed with fire, and the fire will test the quality of each person's work.*

**(1 Corinthians 3:11–13 NIV)**

# RELUCTANT STUDENT

We're in a class we don't want to be in now or ever. We never wanted to be an expert in the end stages of life, not if it meant we had to lose someone we love. But we can't seem to drop this class. We're enrolled for the duration. So, we have decided that we might as well learn all we can while we're here. We sit down to listen, and we ask Him. *What do we need to learn in this class? What are you trying to teach us?* We really want to get this right, so we're listening.

Dear Lord, what are You trying to teach us in this season? We want to learn from You and from the friends around us. We want to be more Christ-like at the end of this course. We don't know when it will end, so we need to be diligent students now. Give us a teachable spirit. We don't know the expectations because there was no course description, so we need Your guidance. There doesn't seem to be any kind of syllabus, so we will have to listen closely for Your instruction. Help us to listen well, Father. Amen.

*Call to me and I will answer you and tell you great and unsearchable things you do not know.*

**(Jeremiah 33:3 NIV)**

*I love the LORD, for he heard my voice; he heard my cry for mercy. Because he turned his ear to me, I will call on him as long as I live.*

**(Psalm 116:1–2 NIV)**

*In the morning, LORD, you hear my voice; in the morning I lay my requests before you and wait expectantly.*

**(Psalm 5:3 NIV)**

*Listen and hear my voice; pay attention and hear what I say.*

**(Isaiah 28:23 NIV)**

*O God, from my youth you have taught me, and I still proclaim Your wondrous deeds.*

**(Psalm 71:17 ESV)**

*Many nations will come and say, "Come and let us go up to the mountain of the LORD and to the temple of the God of Jacob. He will teach us his ways, so that we may walk in his paths."*

**(Micah 4:2a NIV)**

# RECOUNTING GOOD TIMES

Even after our loved ones are gone, our memories with them will be with us for our lifetime. The bad memories seem to fade, and the good times come to the surface. Sights, sounds, smells, tastes can bring recollections to the forefront.

Whenever I taste vanilla ice cream, sweet and powerful memories of my grandmother flood my mind. I can picture sitting on the old ice cream maker as she churned it and anticipating getting to eat some smooth, velvet-like vanilla! Likewise, when I smell permanent wave solutions, I immediately recall my other grandmother who owned a beauty shop. Also, seeing a backyard bench swing reminds me of swinging with my grandfather as he sang me songs from his childhood. I still remember most of those songs. Our memories are lasting and can bring us joy! We have these recollections to carry into eternity when we will see our loved ones again.

Lord, thank you for allowing us to remember sweet times even after our loved ones are gone. You are a God of joy, and You have amazing ways to carry us through any season. Thank you for equipping us in times of trouble. Thank you for letting us hold on to the good and trust You for the rest. Amen.

*For the Lord God is a sun and shield; the Lord bestows favor and honor; no good thing does he withhold from those whose walk is blameless.*

**(Psalm 84:11 NIV)**

*Every good and perfect gift is from above, coming down from the Father of heavenly lights, who does not change like shifting shadows.*

**(James 1:17 NIV)**

*Surely the righteous will never be shaken; they will be remembered forever.*

**(Psalm 112:6 NIV)**

*These days should be remembered and observed in every generation by every family, and in every province and in every city. And these days of Purim should never fail to be celebrated by the Jews—nor should the memory of these days die out among their descendants.*

**(Esther 9:28 NIV)**

I praise you for remembering me in everything and for holding to the traditions just as I passed them on to you.

**(1 Corinthians 11:2 NIV)**

# SELF-TALK

God calls us His 'masterpiece.' There are many days where it is hard to feel like anything close to a masterpiece... we feel more like a master-mess. It is easy to tell ourselves we are not adequate, we are failing, and we should be doing so much more. This self-talk makes us feel negative about ourselves. At these times, we need to fight to believe the truth of who God says we are: God's work of art, adopted by Him, and blessed and not condemned. Replacing our negative self-talk with what God has put in the Bible glorifies God the creator and strengthens our spiritual soul.

Holy Spirit, teach us to recognize when we are telling ourselves things contrary to Your truth. Our thoughts can dilute our days if we let the negative overpower our minds. Help us to know Your Word and to apply it to our lives and thoughts. Remind us of who you say we are. You have good for us, so help us to walk in it. Amen.

*Why, my soul, are you downcast? Why so disturbed within me? Put your hope in God, for I will yet praise him, my Savior and my God.*

**(Psalm 42:5 NIV)**

*Therefore, there is now no condemnation for those who are in Christ Jesus,*

**(Romans 8:1 NIV)**

*For we are God's handiwork, created in Christ Jesus to do good works, which God prepared in advance for us to do.*

**(Ephesians 2:10 NIV)**

*Be careful how you think; your life is shaped by your thoughts.*

**(Proverbs 4:23 GNT)**

*Even if I were innocent, my mouth would condemn me; if I were blameless, it would pronounce me guilty.*

**(Job 9:20 NIV)**

*Finally, brothers, whatever is true, whatever is honorable, whatever is just, whatever is pure, whatever is lovely, whatever is commendable, it there is any excellence, if there is anything worthy of praise, think about these things.*

**(Philippians 4:8 ESV)**

*Peace I leave with you; my peace I give to you. Not as the world gives do I give to you. Let not your hearts be troubled, neither let them be afraid.*

**(John 14:27 ESV)**

# MORNING REFUGE

Finding moments alone with God in the morning can set the tone for our day. This is a common habit taught to Believers, but it seems to be even more important in this season. We need to know God's words of comfort, strength, and compassion to help us survive. We need quiet with Him to infuse us with His peace. It seems that if we don't get some time in the first part of the day to focus on what God's Word says, then the day is swept away from us and it never happens. We have to diligently protect some time to sit with Him because we are frequently called to assist and facilitate helping our loved ones or just keeping up with our tasks, and time quickly vanishes. It's a picture of the illustration of the parent on the airplane, and in the case of a crash, the parent is to put the oxygen mask first on themselves and then on their child. We need to attach to our source before we give out to others. We have to connect ourselves with the breath of God.

Father, help us to keep You as a priority in our schedule. Protect our time with You. We thank You for bringing us strength and providing us with affirmation and inspiration. You are our source in this life. Open up moments that we can spend soaking up Your presence today. Amen.

*The LORD God has given me the tongue of those who are taught, that I may know how to sustain with a word him who is weary. Morning by morning he awakens; he awakens my ear to hear as those who are taught. The LORD God has opened my ear, and I was not rebellious; I turned not backward.*

**(Isaiah 50:4–5 ESV)**

*Satisfy us in the morning with your unfailing love, that we may sing for joy and be glad all our days.*

**(Psalm 90:14 NIV)**

*He who dwells in the shelter of the Most High will abide in the shadow of the Almighty. I will say to the Lord, "My refuge and my fortress, my God, in whom I trust."*

**(Psalm 91:1–2 ESV)**

*The Spirit of God has made me; the breath of the Almighty gives me life.*

**(Job 33:4 NIV)**

# RIGHT SIDE

There are many references in Scripture to God being at our right hand. The right side was thought to be the place of honor. We are to hold God in that highest place of honor in our lives. This means that God comes even before our loved one who we are caring for now. As we face daily decisions, it helps to ask ourselves, What would best honor God in this situation? What is God's call in this instead of what would make others happy? We will undoubtedly have to confront questions with no easy answers, but if He is at our right hand, we will not be shaken.

Lord, some days we feel we cannot discern what the best solutions may be. We need You by our side as our guide and our rock. We want You as the plumb line for our lives so that we can measure options and know how to make choices. Thank you for being with us. Amen.

*I have set the LORD always before me. Because He is at my right hand, I will not be shaken.*

**(Psalm 16:8 ESV)**

47

*The Lord is at your right hand;*

**(Psalm 110:5a NIV)**

*The LORD watches over you—the LORD is your shade at your right hand; the sun will not harm you by day, nor the moon by night. The LORD will keep you from all harm— he will watch over your life; the LORD will watch over your coming and going both now and forevermore.*

**(Psalm 121:5–8 NIV)**

*My soul clings to you; your right hand upholds me.*

**(Psalm 63:8 ESV)**

# DIFFERENT BELIEFS

My faith gives me hope of eternity, but I have a loved one I help care for who has no faith. In fact, he adamantly opposes any belief of an afterlife or a Savior. So, how do we live with radical differences in beliefs between the caregiver and the patient? Our way of coping with the loss of our loved one is to know the hope that we will see them in heaven. How do we bear the loss if we realize they have chosen to deny Christ? It's painful because we hurt for what they are missing; we hurt because of their lack of hope. Still, we keep believing that one day soon, they will make a choice to submit their life to Jesus and to see us in heaven for eternity. We can keep hoping.

Father don't let me give up hope. You are an amazing God, and Your ways are much more complicated and strategic than my ways. Keep calling my loved one to You. Reach out to them. Find them in the midst of their unbelief. Give them the gift of faith before they die. Don't let us lose our hope. Keep us focused on You and Your creative power. Amen.

*Very truly I tell you, the one who believes has
eternal life.*

**(John 6:47 NIV)**

*I am still confident of this: I will see the good-
ness of the LORD in the land of the living.
Wait for the LORD; be strong and take heart
and wait for the LORD.*

**(Psalm 27: 13–14 NIV)**

*In his name the nations will put their hope.*

**(Matthew 12:21 NIV)**

*God did this so that men would seek him
and perhaps reach out for him and find him,
though he is not far from each one of us.*

**(Acts 17:27 NIV)**

*And this is the testimony: God has given us
eternal life, and this life is in his Son.*

**(1 John 5:11 NIV)**

*but whoever denies me before men, I will also
deny him before My Father who is in heaven.*

**(Matthew 10:33 ESV)**

*if we endure, we will also reign with him; if
we disown him, he will also disown us.*

**(2 Timothy 2:12 NIV)**

*I want to know Christ and the power of his
resurrection and the fellowship of sharing in
his sufferings, becoming like him in his death,*

*and so, somehow, to attain to the resurrection from the dead.*

**(Philippians 3:10–11 NIV)**

# SWEET SLEEP

A deep, uninterrupted night's sleep can be so revital-izing. However, in this season, sleep is often sporadic and unpredictable—and hardly refreshing. We can ask the Holy Spirit for refreshment because He is our helper. We can pray for strength in the middle of our fatigue. He will be with us in this valley in life. Our God can restore our soul even when we physically are weary.

*Father, be with us in this season and refresh us even though we may be losing sleep. Thank you for being with us in this unknown territory. Thank you for being our restoration in our time of need. Please bless our sleep and give us Your peace. Amen.*

*The LORD is my shepherd;*

*I have all that I need.*

*He lets me rest in green meadows;*

*he leads me beside peaceful streams.*

*He renews my strength.*

*He guides me along right paths,*

*bringing honor to his name.*

*Even when I walk*

*through the darkest valley,*

*I will not be afraid,*

*for you are close beside me.*

*Your rod and your staff*

*protect and comfort me.*

**(Psalm 23:1–4 NLT)**

*On my bed I remember you; I think of you through the watches of the night. Because you are my help, I sing in the shadow of your wings.*

**(Psalm 63:6–7 NIV)**

*I will lie down and sleep in peace, for you alone, O Lord, make me dwell in safety.*

**(Psalm 4:8 BSB)**

*My son, preserve sound judgment and discernment, do not let them out of your sight; they will be life for you, an ornament to grace your neck. Then you will go on your way in safety, and your foot will not stumble; when you lie down, you will not be afraid; when you lie down, your sleep will be sweet. Have no fear of sudden disaster or of the ruin that overtakes the wicked, for the Lord will be your confidence and will keep your foot from being snared.*

**(Proverbs 3:21–26 NIV)**

*The LORD gives strength to his people; the LORD blesses his people with peace.*

**(Psalm 29:11 NIV)**

# FAIL

Some days are just full of fails. Today was one of them. I was intolerant and irritable as a caregiver. We all have days or portions of days like this. We feel terrible afterward. We look back and wonder how we could have been so impatient. What must the Lord feel as He looks at us and sees our shortcomings? He has every right to be irritable with us, but He looks at us with grace and mercy. As long as we can learn from our failures, it is not wasted. If we think of a baby trying to learn to walk, he learns from each attempt until he can finally walk anywhere. Some days feel like we have begun at the beginning. What can we learn from this day in order to walk a little better in the future?

Lord, we failed today. We're so sorry. Please forgive us. We don't want to be impatient. We need Your grace to refine us and deepen us. Only through Your strength can we walk this road. Teach us how to have more mercy and make fewer mistakes. Amen.

*Get rid of all bitterness, rage and anger, brawling and slander, along with every form of malice. Be kind and compassionate to one another, forgiving each other, just as in Christ God forgave you.*

**(Ephesians 4:31–32 NIV)**

*Repent, then, and turn to God, so that your sins may be wiped out, that times of refreshing may come from the Lord,*

**(Acts 3:19 NIV)**

*Therefore, if anyone is in Christ, he is a new creation; the old has gone, the new has here!*

**(2 Corinthians 5:17 NIV)**

*Be kind and compassionate to one another, forgiving each other, just as in Christ God forgave you. Be imitators of God, therefore, as dearly loved children and live a life of love, just as Christ loved us and gave himself up for us as a fragrant offering and sacrifice to God.*

**(Ephesians 4:32–5:2 NIV)**

*He has showed you, O mortal, what is good. And what does the LORD require of you? To act justly and to love mercy and to walk humbly with your God.*

**(Micah 6:8 NIV)**

# TRIALS ARE PROMISED

In the Bible, the wording is clear that we will face trials. We sometimes think that our lives are supposed to be smooth sailing, or at least easier than it is right now. We get deceived into the thoughts that if our lives have adversity, something is just not fair! However, God wanted us to face life knowing that we would have persecutions and difficulties. He wanted us to let the struggle refine us, but He also promises us that He will never leave us. No matter what we are experiencing today, He is with us in difficulty. Our Father can make something good out of our trials.

Lord, help me look at my difficult situations like a natural part of this life, and then use them to create more of Your character in me. Help me recognize quickly that You are not punishing me, but that this life just has natural consequences, but You can teach us through the trials. Use this time to teach me more about You. Amen.

*Consider it pure joy, my brothers and sisters, whenever you face trials of many kinds, because you know that the testing of your faith produces perseverance. Let perseverance finish its work so that you may be mature and complete, not lacking anything. If any of you lacks wisdom, you should ask God, who gives generously to all without finding fault, and it will be given to you.*

**(James 1:2–5 NIV)**

*My son, if you accept my words and store up my commands within you, turning your ear to wisdom and applying your heart to understanding— indeed, if you call out for insight and cry aloud for understanding, and if you look for it as for silver and search for it as for hidden treasure, then you will understand the fear of the Lord and find the knowledge of God. For the Lord gives wisdom; from his mouth come knowledge and understanding.*

**(Proverbs 2:1–6 NIV)**

*I know what it is to be in need, and I know what it is to have plenty. I have learned the secret of being content in any and every situation, whether well fed or hungry, whether living in plenty or in want. I can do all this through him who gives me strength.*

**(Philippians 4:12–13 NIV)**

*And the God of all grace, who called you to his eternal glory in Christ, after you have suffered a little while, will himself restore you and make you strong, firm and steadfast.*

**(1 Peter 5:10 NIV)**

# BUCKLE UP

We've hit a downturn in this roller-coaster. The crucial safety step in riding an amusement ride is to buckle your seat belt before the ride begins. What we have to remember is that some riders are sent through corkscrews, backward plunges, deep tunnels, loops, and other wild trails... and sometimes life takes us through these unexpected directions too. So, what can we do? Nothing but ride it out as our seat belt is securely fastened. What does that look like? It is wise to have established habits in our lives before we hit a downward spiral. This protective "seat belt" can be habits such as: eating a nourishing and well-balanced diet, taking care of ourselves physically with plenty of sleep and exercise, investing time in our spiritual health by prayer and replenishing input from God's Word, and surrounding ourselves with people who support us well. Even if you did not have these in place before, we can set them in place now to some extent. Remember to hold on to the Father's promises and buckle up!

Dear Father, we are hanging on tight and trusting in You as we enter this downturn. Help us to be diligent in taking care of ourselves as we take care of others. Protect our time with You in this busy season. Hold on to us as we hold on to You. In Jesus Name, Amen.

*So, whether you eat or drink, or whatever you do, do all to the glory of God.*

**(1 Corinthians 10:31 ESV)**

*Beloved, I pray that all may go well with you and that you may be in good health, as it goes well with your soul.*

**(3 John 1:2 ESV)**

*I appeal to you therefore, brothers, by the mercies of God, to present your bodies as a living sacrifice, holy and acceptable to God, which is your spiritual worship.*

**(Romans 12:1 ESV)**

*But he answered, "It is written, 'Man shall not live by bread alone, but by every word that comes from the mouth of God.'"*

**(Matthew 4:4 ESV)**

*I have said these things to you, that in me you may have peace. In the world you will have tribulation. But take heart; I have overcome the world.*

**(John 16:33 ESV)**

*My soul clings to you; your right hand up-holds me.*

**(Psalm 63:8 ESV)**

*Sovereign Lord, you are God! Your covenant is trustworthy, and you have promised these good things to your servant.*

**(2 Samuel 7:28 NIV)**

*Those who know your name will trust in you, for you, LORD, have never forsaken those who seek you.*

**(Psalm 9:10 NIV)**

*The king was overjoyed and gave orders to lift Daniel out of the den. And when Daniel was lifted from the den, no wound was found on him, because he had trusted in his God.*

**(Daniel 6:23 NIV)**

# FAMILY

What can you do if your family disagrees about care issues with your loved one? It is disappointing and discouraging to have to battle different opinions while at the same time dealing with your loved one's health issues. Not one of us is completely right in our opinions. Each of us is trying to do our best with the information we have, and this best may not be identical. We have to be willing to let go of the details that are non-critical and only battle for the things that really matter. Ask God to give you His perspective on things and to honor each other in the process.

Dear Lord, help me to have the humility to understand that others may not agree with me. Let me see them through Your eyes and love them. Give me Your wisdom as I walk through this season. May I be the fragrance of Christ today. Amen.

*But thanks be to God, who always leads us as captives in Christ's triumphal procession and uses us to spread the aroma of the knowledge of him everywhere.*

**(2 Corinthians 2:14 NIV)**

*But he gives more grace. That is why Scripture says, "God opposes the proud, but gives grace to the humble."*

**(James 4:6 NIV)**

*For everyone who exalts himself will be humbled, and he who humbles himself will be exalted.*

**(Luke 14:11 ESV)**

*The reward for humility and fear of the LORD is riches and honor and life.*

**(Proverbs 22:4 ESV)**

# PREDICTIONS

There is not a way to predict the future with 100 percent accuracy. Our lives would be so different if we could know about things to come and know the path marked out for us. For example, when running a marathon, you know the set distance and you have information markers all along the path guiding your way. There are usually no surprises. You know how long your route will be, the distance you have completed, and how many miles until the finish line. Life, however, is not so neatly organized and calculable. There are some events in our lives which we can depend on happening in a definite order, but other things cannot be foreseen. Most caregiving cannot be programmed or mapped out ahead of time. We can put some plans into place, but there has to be a fluidity to our system. The good news is that God can use these times of flexibility to teach us great things and mold us into His likeness. It is less stressful if we remember to hold our plans loosely because we cannot predict all that will happen, and our scenario may need to change.

Father, this seems like an unmarked path we are on. We need You more than ever. Give us encouragement when we are low and help us to live with your peace during this journey. You are the God of hope, so we look to You for our hope now. Amen.

*May our Lord Jesus Christ himself and God our Father, who loved us and by his grace gave us eternal encouragement and good hope, encourage your hearts and strengthen you in every good deed and word.*

**(2 Thessalonians 2:16–17 NIV)**

*The LORD himself goes before you and will be with you; he will never leave you nor forsake you. Do not be afraid; do not be discouraged.*

**(Deuteronomy 31:8 NIV)**

*But I trust in you, LORD; I say, "You are my God."*

**(Psalm 31:14 NIV)**

*May the God of hope fill you with all joy and peace as you trust in him, so that you may overflow with hope by the power of the Holy Spirit.*

**(Romans 15:13 NIV)**

*In their hearts humans plan their course, but the Lord establishes his steps.*

**(Proverbs 16:9 NIV)**

# MAGNIFYING GLASS

Sometimes we have to look at our motives and our choices with a different eye. It takes an effort to step away from our caregiving situation and re-evaluate issues. On occasion, it helps to come back and visit the questions, *How can we best give our loved ones quality in this season of life? Are our choices for our loved ones extending life or just delaying death?* Extending life would mean that quality living is still happening. Delaying death would be more defined as still physically alive, but mentally and emotionally, things have stalled or even stopped. It is a tough call but a sensible time to gather input from others who professionally deal with illnesses and end-of-life issues. We need each other, and caregiving requires a team approach. Don't be hesitant to ask others and to pray for a wise perspective.

Dear Lord, we have not walked this path before. Bring people into our lives who will give us wise counsel. Teach us to work with others and to accept help. We give control to You. Thank You for being our light on this path. Amen.

*Where there is no [wise, intelligent] guidance, the people fall [and go off course like a ship without a helm], but in the abundance of [wise and godly] counselors there is victory.*

**(Proverbs 11:14 AMP)**

*I will instruct you and teach you in the way you should go; I will counsel you with my eye upon you.*

**(Psalm 32:8 ESV)**

*Plans fail for lack of counsel, but with many advisers they succeed.*

**(Proverbs 15:22 NIV)**

*Listen to advice and accept instruction, that you may gain wisdom in the future.*

**(Proverbs 19:20 ESV)**

# IT'S WORTH IT

Grief is the price you pay for loving someone, so in the scheme of things it is worth it. We'd rather have loved them for a little while than to have not loved them at all. We understand that part of feeling deeply for another person means those feelings include our whole range of emotions... joy, delight, frustration, fear, and grief. When we love the person we care for, then seeing them decline tugs at us at a painfully deep emotional level. However, if we think about never having had them in our lives, we realize that the pain of seeing them need care at this stage is well worth the cost. Having them in our lives has been a rare treasure, and knowing this helps us walk through this grieving season.

Lord, we are blessed by our loved ones and how they touched our lives. Thank you for putting them in our lives. It is difficult to face letting them go. We have shared such joy with them! Now we are walking in the valley of the shadow of death, and we really need Your presence. Be with us in this season. Remind us of the sweet memories we will carry with us to comfort us. Holy Spirit, bring Your comfort. Amen.

*Beloved, let us love one another, for love is from God, and whoever loves has been born of God and knows God. Anyone who does not love does not know God, because God is love.*

**(1 John 4:7–8 ESV)**

*Greater love has no one than this, that someone lay down his life for his friends.*

**(John 15:13 ESV)**

*Truly, truly, I say to you, unless a grain of wheat falls into the earth and dies, it remains alone; but if it dies, it bears much fruit.*

**(John 12:24 ESV)**

*Praise be to the God and Father of our Lord Jesus Christ, the Father of compassion and the God of all comfort, who comforts us in all our troubles, so that we can comfort those in any trouble with the comfort we ourselves receive from God.*

**(2 Corinthians 1:3–4 NIV)**

*And everyone who lives and believes in me shall never die. Do you believe this?*

**(John 11:26 ESV)**

# BE REAL

We are not the one who needs the caregiving, or are we? We get so busy taking into consideration all of the needs of our loved one that we can forget what our needs are too. It is important to have a close circle of friends with ~~who~~ *whom* we can be real with at any time. Genuineness and transparency with others who encourage and support us are vital to our care. Paul often spoke in his letters in the Bible about Believers who helped him on his journeys and in prison. We are called to encourage each other!

> Father, it is difficult to open up our lives to other people. Help us to call on others to walk with us. Bring people to us who will encourage us in our faith and our journey. Let us also be that support to others who may need it. Amen.

> *I commend to you our sister Phoebe, a servant of the church at Cenchreae, that you may welcome her in the Lord in a way worthy of the saints, and help her in whatever she may*

*need from you, for she has been a patron of
many and of myself as well.*

**(Romans 16:1–2 ESV)**

*When Job's three friends, Eliphaz the
Temanite, Bildad the Shuhite and Zophar the
Naamathite, heard about all the troubles that
had come upon him, they set out from their
homes and met together by agreement to go
and sympathize with him and comfort him.*

**(Job 2:11 NIV)**

*Two are better than one, because they have
a good return for their labor: If either of
them falls down, one can help the other up.
But pity anyone who falls and has no one to
help them up. Also, if two lie down together,
they will keep warm. But how can one keep
warm alone? Though one may be overpow-
ered, two can defend themselves. A cord of
three strands is not quickly broken.*

**(Ecclesiastes 4:9–12 NIV)**

*Therefore, as God's chosen people, holy and
dearly loved, clothe yourselves with compassion, kindness, humility, gentleness and patience.*

**(Colossians 3:12 NIV)**

*Therefore, encourage and comfort one an-
other and build up one another, just as you
are now doing.*

**(1 Thessalonians 5:11 AMP)**

*Above all, love each other deeply, because
love covers over a multitude of sins. Offer
hospitality to one another without grum-
bling. Each of you should use whatever gift
you have received to serve others, as faithful stewards of God's grace in its various
forms.*

**(1 Peter 4:8–10 NIV)**

*I long to see you so that I may impart to you
some spiritual gift to make you strong—that
is, that you and I may be mutually encouraged by each other's faith.*

**(Romans 1:11–12 NIV)**

# COURAGE

Some days it just takes courage to put one foot in front of the other and keep going. It's kind of like walking into a dark cave, not knowing for sure what you are putting your foot down on with each step. You tend to carefully feel around with your foot before you place it down to carry your weight. Sometimes you misjudge, and your foot gets stuck in a hole, so you have to pull it back out quickly... again! But you need courage to keep going and to move forward. Courage can be defined as strength in the face of pain or grief. No step is necessarily easy, but our source of strength is from our relationship with Jesus. We can depend on Him to give us the courage to keep going.

Father, I don't know what lies ahead of me this day. Give me Your resilience to walk today out. Help me to honor all who come in my path. Help me to know which choices to make. Thank you for your strength. Amen.

*I can do all this through him who gives me strength.*

**(Philippians 4:13 NIV)**

79

*David also said to Solomon his son, "Be strong and courageous, and do the work. Do not be afraid or discouraged, for the LORD God, my God, is with you. He will not fail you or forsake you until all the work for the service of the temple of the LORD is finished.*

**(1 Chronicles 28:20 NIV)**

*Be strong and courageous. Do not be afraid or terrified because of them, for the LORD your God goes with you; he will never leave you nor forsake you.*

**(Deuteronomy 31:6 NIV)**

*So do not fear, for I am with you; do not be dismayed, for I am your God. I will strengthen you and help you; I will uphold you with my righteous right hand.*

**(Isaiah 41:10 NIV)**

# FORGIVENESS = FREEDOM

You may have had painful things which were done to you by your loved one, and you have a hope that one day they will come to you and be remorseful for what they did and ask your forgiveness. If that happens, you are so fortunate! What a gift! But in some families, the perpetrator of the wound may never acknowledge it, and this hurt may never be corrected. How disappointing it is that you will never hear them say, "I'm sorry." Especially when you may be the caregiver for this person, and you hope each day might be the day they show remorse. But if it never happens, how do you offload your resentment, disappointment, and hurt? In prayer to Christ, by yourself or with a friend, tell Him all your hurts and then "hand" them to Him. Submit your wounds to Christ to heal. Over the next few months, continue to say, "Lord, I gave that to You, and in return, I ask for healing. I believe Your Word and Your power to heal."

Father, You know how we have been wounded. We hoped it would have been righted, but we see it may not happen. You tell us that You heal wounds and that You carry our burdens. Lord, this burden is not one I want to carry any longer. I ask forgiveness for any resentment or bitterness which I have carried. I release this person, and I submit it all to You. I know You are God, and You will handle this better than I could. Help me heal. Amen.

*The Spirit of the Sovereign LORD is on me, because the LORD has anointed me to proclaim good news to the poor. He has sent me to bind up the brokenhearted, to proclaim freedom for the captives, and release from darkness for the prisoners, to proclaim the year of the LORD's favor and the day of vengeance of our God, to comfort all who mourn, and provide for those who grieve in Zion—to bestow on them a crown of beauty instead of ashes, the oil of joy instead of mourning, and a garment of praise instead of despair. They will be called oaks of righteousness, a planting of the LORD for the display of his splendor.*

**(Isaiah 61:1–3 NIV)**

*I will come down and speak with you there, and I will take some of the power of the Spirit that is on you and put it on them. They will share the burden of the people with you so that you will not have to carry it alone.*

**(Numbers 11:17 NIV)**

*Come to Me, all you who are weary and burdened, and I will give you rest.*

**(Matthew 11:28 NIV)**

*And my God will meet all your needs according to the riches of his glory in Christ Jesus.*

**(Philippians 4:19 NIV)**

*Surely he took up our pain and bore our suffering, yet we considered him punished by God, stricken by him, and afflicted. But he was pierced for our transgressions, he was crushed for our iniquities; the punishment that brought us peace was on him, and by his wounds we are healed.*

**(Isaiah 53:4–5 NIV)**

*He heals the brokenhearted and binds up their wounds.*

**(Psalm 147:3 NIV)**

*Therefore confess your sins to each other and pray for each other so that you may be healed. The prayer of a righteous man is powerful and effective.*

**(James 5:16 NIV)**

# DO IT NOW!

What do you want to be sure to do for your loved one before they are gone? Why not do it now? Are there things on their "bucket list" that you could possibly help them do still? Even little things are important. A wise friend shared that she never regrets the things she did for her mother-in-law before she died. She only wishes she had done more. For example, she shared that her mother-in-law really wanted tacos, and so she brought her tacos for lunch. However, she now looks back and says, "Why didn't I take her with me to pick out her tacos? She would have loved that!" This is such a small thing, but apparently, a big deal since she still thinks of it. What is there in the lives of our loved ones that we could do now which would bring them great joy? We can even ask them for ideas, as well as thinking of what they enjoyed when they were independent.

Lord, show us ways to bring joy into the lives of those we take care of in this season. Give us Your eyes to understand what would delight them. We cannot comprehend what they must be going through right now. Teach us compassion so we can be Your hands and feet to our loved ones. Amen.

*Praise be to the God and Father of our Lord Jesus Christ, the Father of compassion and the God of all comfort, who comforts us in all our troubles, so that we can comfort those in any trouble with the comfort we ourselves receive from God.*

**(2 Corinthians 1:3–4 NIV)**

*Your love has given me great joy and encouragement, because you, brother, have refreshed the hearts of the Lord's saints.*

**(Philemon 1:7 NIV)**

*By this all people will know that you are my disciples, if you have love for one another.*

**(John 13:35 ESV)**

*Each of you should use whatever gift you have received to serve others, as faithful stewards of God's grace in its various forms.*

**(1 Peter 4:10 NIV)**

*Shout for joy, you heavens; rejoice, you earth; burst into song, you mountains! For the LORD comforts his people and will have compassion on his afflicted ones.*

**(Isaiah 49:13 NIV)**

*The LORD is gracious and righteous; our God is full of compassion.*

**(Psalm 116:5 NIV)**

*Though you have not seen him, you love him; and even though you do not see him now, you believe in him and are filled with an inexpressible and glorious joy, for you are receiving the goal of your faith, the salvation of your souls.*

**(1 Peter 1:8–9 NIV)**

*Nehemiah said, "Go and enjoy choice food and sweet drinks, and send some to those who have nothing prepared. This day is sacred to our Lord. Do not grieve, for the joy of the LORD is your strength.*

**(Nehemiah 8:10 NIV)**

# STRETCHING

Stretching can be thought of as expanding or pushing out on our limits for the purpose of making us stronger, more flexible, or more adaptable. This has been a season of stretching. We know that it is developing in us a greater capacity to grow deeper in character. Times of growth are not easy or painless. An athlete knows the importance of stretching and improving muscle flexibility in order to achieve their goal. Now our goal is to become more Christlike, and we can choose to be thankful for the difficult season which is stretching our character. Our Father knows our future, and He is now stretching us and equipping us for what is to come.

Dear Lord, help us to choose thankfulness as we are being stretched. Use this season to mold us into Your likeness. We want the character of Christ. This is a difficult stage in life, but we know that You are with us and our strength comes from You. Amen.

*Dear friends, now we are children of God, and what we will be has not yet been made known. But we know that when Christ appears, we shall be like him, for we shall see him as he is. All who have this hope in him purify themselves, just as he is pure.*

**(1 John 3:2–3 NIV)**

*For this very reason, make every effort to add to your faith goodness; and to goodness, knowledge; and to knowledge, self-control; and to self-control, perseverance; and to perseverance, godliness; and to godliness, mutual affection; and to mutual affection, love. For if you possess these qualities in increasing measure, they will keep you from being ineffective and unproductive in your knowledge of our Lord Jesus Christ.*

**(2 Peter 1:5–8 NIV)**

*And we know that in all things God works for the good of those who love him, who have been called according to his purpose. For those God foreknew he also predestined to be conformed to the image of his Son, that he might be the firstborn among many brothers and sisters.*

**(Romans 8:28–29 NIV)**

*Follow God's example, therefore, as dearly loved children and walk in the way of love, just as Christ loved us and gave himself up for us as a fragrant offering and sacrifice to God.*

**(Ephesians 5:1–2 NIV)**

*Brothers, I do not consider that I have made it my own. But one thing I do: forgetting what lies behind and straining forward to what lies ahead, I press on toward the goal for the prize of the upward call of God in Christ Jesus.*

**(Philippians 3:13–14 ESV)**

# LET DOWN

When caring for someone else, we cannot foresee all the unexpected things which will be required of us each day. Our days are usually unpredictable. This makes it problematic to follow through with obligations or appointments with other friends and work. Sometimes we feel like we are letting everyone else in our lives down, and we know they may assume it is due to us being irresponsible or unorganized—when in reality, we are battling with unattainable requirements in this season. Our friends just cannot comprehend our days, but God knows. We must remember that He knows we are serving and showing compassion to one of His children, and He looks at us with grace. He sees, and He delights in us!

Lord, help me remember that You know how our days run. You see our heart and understand, even when we disappoint others. May our friends be gifted with extra mercy towards us in this caregiving season. Thank you for delighting in us in whatever season we are in! Amen.

*For the LORD takes delight in His people; He crowns the humble with victory.*

**(Psalm 149:4 NIV)**

*but let him who boasts boast in this, that he understands and knows me, that I am the LORD who practices steadfast love, justice, and righteousness in the earth; for in these things I delight, declares the LORD."*

**(Jeremiah 9:24 ESV)**

*But Samuel replied: "Does the LORD delight in burnt offerings and sacrifices as much as in obeying the LORD? To obey is better than sacrifice, and to heed is better than the fat of rams.*

**(1 Samuel 15:22 NIV)**

*Glory to God in the highest heaven, and on earth peace to those on whom his favor rests.*

**(Luke 2:14 NIV)**

# A NEW PROFESSION

When we are a caregiver for another person, we often have to give up or cut down on our workload in order to have time to take responsibility for our loved one. We have to lay down what may have been the focus of our lives so that we can direct our energies to our loved one more completely. This is a shift in our lives, and the major change can be challenging. There is a change in how society labels or identifies us if we "no longer work." You shift from being a "teacher" or a "businessman" to being described as "not working any longer" or "just staying home to care for family." If we can keep our mindset directed toward Jesus calling us to lay down our lives for others and telling us that to carry each other's burdens fulfills the law of Christ, then we rest knowing we are fulfilling what our greatest supervisor has set before us to accomplish.

Dear Lord, help us to remember that our identity is in You and not in a career or a job. Let us see our role now as a caregiver as a calling from You. You ask us to lay down our lives for You, and this may not be how we expected it to look, but we want to be obedient. Teach us how this walk looks and how to submit our lives fully to You. Our identity comes from You, Father, as You have adopted us and call us by name. Help us to keep that at the forefront of our minds. Amen.

*Carry each other's burdens, and in this way you will fulfill the law of Christ.*

**(Galatians 6:2 NIV)**

*This is my commandment, that you love one another as I loved you. Greater love has no one than this, that he lay down his life for his friends.*

**(John 15:12–13 ESV)**

*Anyone who does not provide for their relatives, and especially for their own household, has denied the faith and is worse than an unbeliever.*

**(1 Timothy 5:8 NIV)**

*For those who are led by the Spirit of God are the children of God. The Spirit you received does not make you slaves, so that you live in fear again; rather, the Spirit you received brought about your adoption to sonship. And by him we cry, "Abba, Father."*

**(Romans 8:14–15 NIV)**

*So in Christ Jesus you are all children of God through faith, for all of you who were baptized into Christ have clothed yourselves with Christ.*

**(Galatians 3:26–27 NIV)**

# EMOTIONAL FLARES

Most of our days we are the responsible ones who are in control and orchestrating our lives and the life of our loved one. We are quite adept at keeping things going. However, unexpectedly, it seems emotions can hit us out of nowhere, and it surprises even us! We have to allow ourselves to grieve when it shows up because this is a sign that emotions need to be expressed. We may be checking out at a store and something reminds us of what we used to love to do with our family member who we care for, and a deep sadness overtakes us. That's ok, and it is part of the process. We have experienced a loss, and we need to acknowledge that by crying, by talking to a friend, or by writing about it. We need to give ourselves permission to grieve as it comes. Being emotional is not a weakness but a normal human way to deal with our losses. Jesus understands what you are going through.

Father, we realize the things we miss with our loved ones. We feel the losses. It is difficult to process this sometimes because this is happening in stages. We know that You lived through grief, and You understand. Comfort us, Holy Spirit, as we give our sadness to You. Amen.

*He was despised and rejected by men, a man of sorrows and acquainted with grief;*

**(Isaiah 53:3a ESV)**

*Blessed are those who mourn, for they shall be comforted.*

**(Matthew 5:4 ESV)**

*He heals the brokenhearted and binds up their wounds.*

**(Psalm 147:3 ESV)**

*Blessed be the God and Father of our Lord Jesus Christ, the Father of mercies and God of all comfort, who comforts us in all our affliction, so that we may be able to comfort those who are in any affliction, with the comfort with which we ourselves are comforted by God.*

**(2 Corinthians 1:3–4 ESV)**

*The LORD is near to those who are discouraged; he saves those who have lost all hope.*

**(Psalm 34:18 GNT)**

*May God, the source of hope, fill you with all joy and peace by means of your faith in him, so that your hope will continue to grow by the power of the Holy Spirit.*

**(Romans 15:13 GNT)**

# RED TAPE

When we began this caregiving process, we did not think about all the paperwork and red tape that would accompany our role. We possibly have had to learn about DNRs, Living Wills, Power of Attorneys, wills, insurance details, Medicare, and on and on. Much of this can be overwhelming. We need to remember that it is acceptable to find others to help us. There may be people in your life who have walked this path already and can simplify so many details. It takes humility and boldness to ask for advice, but the Bible encourages us to seek wise counsel.

*Father, sometimes we feel like we cannot possibly know the answers, and we have so much new information to wade through. It is not our human nature to humble ourselves and ask for help, so mold us to be teachable. Bring wise counselors to us. We can depend on You and Your people, and we do not have to take this all on ourselves. We realize this and are thankful. Amen.*

*Where there is no guidance the people fall.
But in abundance of counselors there is victory.*

**(Proverbs 11:14 NASB 1995)**

*The way of a fool is right in his own eyes, but a wise man is he who listens to counsel.*

**(Proverbs 12:15 NASB 1995)**

*Therefore, O king, may my advice be pleasing to you: break away now from your sins by doing righteousness and from your iniquities by showing mercy to the poor, in case there may be a prolonging of your prosperity.'*

**(Daniel 4:27 NASB 1995)**

*But God has put the body together, giving greater honor to the parts that lacked it, so that there should be no division in the body, but that its parts should have equal concern for each other.*

**(1 Corinthians 12:24b–25 NIV)**

*Who is wise and understanding among you? Let them show it by their good life, by deeds done in the humility that comes from wisdom.*

**(James 3:13 NIV)**

*Good and upright is the LORD; therefore he instructs sinners in his ways. He guides the humble in what is right and teaches them his way.*

**(Psalm 25:8–9 NIV)**

# MEDICATION MIX-UPS

There may come a time when your loved one can no longer make the right judgment calls. Some may willingly give up their daily prescription tasks, while others may fight you regarding their ability to continue to oversee their medications. Part of the problem comes because the loved one may not objectively see themselves and their shortcomings, so they honestly think they can handle things as they used to do. It is a very difficult position to be in when you have to assert the power to take over any of their personal chores. Just as with our children, some decisions we make will not be favorable, but we still have to follow through. We need to remember that God says the correction is for our good and that it is a sign we are blessed. We only take over these things for our loved one because we love them, care about their health, and want it done correctly. It is for their good.

Dear Father, help us to watch over our loved ones well. Keep reminding us of the main goal to honor them and to care for them even when they do not like what we do. Encourage us in this season and help us to encourage them. Amen.

*Keep watch over yourselves and all the flock of which the Holy Spirit has made you overseers. Be shepherds of the church of God, which he bought with his own blood.*

**(Acts 20:28 NIV)**

*Whoever disregards discipline comes to poverty and shame, but whoever heeds correction is honored.*

**(Proverbs 13:18 NIV)**

*Those who disregard discipline despise themselves, but the one who heeds correction gains understanding.*

**(Proverbs 15:32 NIV)**

*Listen to advice and accept discipline, and at the end you will be counted among the wise.*

**(Proverbs 19:20 NIV)**

*For lack of discipline they will die, led astray by their own great folly.*

**(Proverbs 5:23 NIV)**

*After all, no one ever hated their own body, but they feed and care for their body, just as Christ does the church—*

**(Ephesians 5:29 NIV)**

*The LORD will keep you from all harm— he will watch over your life; the LORD will watch over your coming and going both now and forevermore.*

**(Psalm 121:7–8 NIV)**

*And there were shepherds living out in the fields nearby, keeping watch over their flocks at night.*

**(Luke 2:8 NIV)**

# LOOK AROUND

There are so many big activities going on in our lives that we may forget to notice the little things around us. These small happenings or items can be hidden blessings that we only need to look for more closely. For example, are there flowers outside your door to enjoy? Do you have birds nesting in your trees that you can observe? Is there something about the weather you can enjoy? Pay attention to your environment and seek out what you can be thankful for now. Ask the Lord to help make you more aware of the blessings in your day. The more you look around, the more you will notice.

Dear Lord, keep my focus on You and Your creation. Lift my head to see the beauty of Your handiwork and to be reminded that You have good things for me today. Thank you for Your faithfulness in sharing Your blessings with me. Amen.

*...The heavens are telling of the glory of God; And their expanse is declaring the work of his hands.*

(Psalm 19:1 NASB 1995)

*God saw all that He had made, and behold, it was very good. And there was evening and there was morning, the sixth day.*

(Genesis 1:31 NASB 1995)

*For since the creation of the world His invisible attributes, His eternal power and divine nature, have been clearly seen, being understood through what has been made, so that they are without excuse.*

(Romans 1:20 NASB 1995)

*And when they heard this, they lifted their voices to God with one accord and said, "O Lord, it is You who MADE THE HEAVEN AND THE EARTH AND THE SEA, AND ALL THAT IS IN THEM,*

(Acts 4:24 NASB 1995)

# WARNING SIGNS

Oftentimes when we focus on someone else's health, we neglect our own. Warning signs may pop up, which alert us that changes need to be made. Some signs to be aware of...

- jaw pain (which can be from stress-related teeth grinding)
- strange and disturbing dreams
- unrestful sleep or insomnia
- disinterest in things you used to enjoy
- intestinal issues
- high blood pressure
- frequent headaches
- hopelessness
- unexplained weight change
- hair loss
- weakened immune system, etc.

These signs give us valuable information and usually require us to alter some things we are doing in our lives. We should be watching for these and ask the Lord to keep us from ignoring them. We can additionally ask close friends or family to let us know if they perceive anything off balance in our lives.

Dear Lord, help us to pay attention to signs You may be giving us to take care of our health. We get so caught up in the details of our loved ones' care that we overlook our issues. Teach us to be open to our friends who care about us and their input. Thank you for giving us signs to alert us of problems. Amen.

*Make me know your ways, O LORD; Teach me your paths. Lead me in your truth and teach me, for you are the God of my salvation; for you I wait all day long.*

**(Psalm 25:4–5 ESV)**

*For you are my rock and my fortress and for your name's sake you will lead me and guide me;*

**(Psalm 31:3 ESV)**

*Let me hear Your faithfulness in the morning; For I trust in You; Teach me the way in which I should walk; For to You I lift up my soul.*

**(Psalm 143:8 NASB)**

*Therefore I urge you, brothers and sisters, by the mercies of God, to present your bodies a living and holy sacrifice, acceptable to God, which is your spiritual service of worship.*

**(Romans 12:1 NASB)**

# EMBRACING THE GOOD DAYS

Today was a good day. These have become so unusual that it is rather surprising now. We need to be sure to embrace the present moments and relish what good has happened at the time it occurs. Living in the moment is common sense, but yet so often, we quickly rush on to the next event or mentally contemplate what is coming in the future and don't stop to enjoy the now. We can teach ourselves to be grateful for this good day. We need to remember to savor the most out of each day and be thankful for it.

Dear Lord, thank you for this day. It was refreshing to experience the good of today. You are an amazing Father who knows how to look after His children, and You blessed us with some sweet moments today. We love You. Amen.

*Even now, take your stand and see this great thing which the LORD is going to do before your eyes.*

**(1 Samuel 12:16 NASB)**

111

*For everything created by God is good, and nothing is to be rejected if it is received with gratitude;*

**(1 Timothy 4:4 NASB)**

*The LORD is good to all, and his mercy is over all that he has made.*

**(Psalm 145:9 ESV)**

*Every good and every perfect gift is from above, coming down from the Father of lights with whom there is no variation or shadow due to change.*

**(James 1:17 ESV)**

*This is the day which the LORD has made; Let us rejoice and be glad in it.*

**(Psalm 118:24 NASB 1995)**

*Taste and see that the LORD is good; blessed is the one who takes refuge in him.*

**(Psalm 34:8 NIV)**

# HITTING THE WALL

There are some days when you feel you have just hit a wall. There is no energy you can muster up to keep on going. Your brain almost goes numb, and you have a hard time making even simple decisions. Little things that were not difficult before become overwhelming. We must find a way to get out of our depleted state for even small moments when we realize that we have face-planted into our walls. Ask God for ideas to restore your soul. Get creative for ways to get refreshed. Consider getting outside for a walk because being outside is therapeutic. You may want to turn on your happy music and dance as physical movement is good for your soul. Or possibly, find someone to stay with your loved one and get away for a few hours or a night.

Lord, we can't do this without You. Teach us ways to walk when we feel we've hit a dead end. Show us things that will bring joy to our souls. Your Presence brings light into darkness, and Your hope shows us ways out of the darkness. We depend on You, dear Father. Amen.

*Serve the Lord with gladness; Come before Him with joyful singing. Know that the LORD Himself is God; It is He who has made us, and not we ourselves; We are His people and the sheep of His pasture. Enter His gates with thanksgiving And His courts with praise. Give thanks to Him, bless His name*

**(Psalm 100:2–4 NASB 1995)**

*You have turned my mourning into dancing; You have loosed my sackcloth and girded me with gladness*

**(Psalm 30:11 NASB 1995)**

*...The heavens declare the glory of God; the skies proclaim the work of his hands.*

**(Psalm 19:1 NIV)**

*"Come to me, all you who are weary and burdened, and I will give you rest.*

**(Matthew 11:28 NIV)**

*For I have satiated the weary soul, and every sorrowful soul have I replenished.*

**(Jeremiah 31:25 ASV)**

*"Come, all you who are thirsty, come to the waters; and you who have no money, come, buy and eat! Come, buy wine and milk without money and without cost.*

**(Isaiah 55:1 NIV)**

# WE STAND FIRM

A hurricane recently hit the coast of Texas, and one town was almost totally demolished. Few buildings or homes remained. One home which stood with very little damage was a house that had been built specifically to withstand hurricane winds. The blueprints of the home included a whole grid of building techniques to keep the structure from damage should gale forces hit. The key to its survival was that the preparations to fortify it was made ahead of time. The home had a whole system of techniques in place to hold it together. In life, we need to have the Bible as our blueprint, and we need to already have in place our grid before a storm arrives. It helps if we can have a firm foundation in the Word of God, a support system of the Body of Christ, and a relationship with the Creator in order to pull through the difficult season we are faced with when caring for a loved one. What will help us to stand firm in the midst of a storm? How can we shore up our foundation?

Dear Lord, please show us the places where our foundation is weak. Teach us to use the wisdom in Your Word to help us through this time.

Gather the Body of Christ around us and help them know how to minister to us. Send Your Holy Spirit to be Your Presence with us on earth. Amen.

*Therefore everyone who hears these words of mine an puts them into practice is like a wise man who built his house on the rock. The rain came down, the streams rose, and the winds blew and beat against that house; yet it did not fall, because it had its foundation on the rock. But everyone who hears these words of mine and does not put them into practice is like a foolish man who built his house on sand. The rain came down, the streams rose, and the winds blew and beat against that house, and it fell with a great crash.*

**(Matthew 7:24–27 NIV)**

*Some trust in chariots and some in horses, but we trust in the name of the LORD our God. They are brought to their knees and fall, but we rise up and stand firm.*

**(Psalm 20:7–8 NIV)**

*Therefore thus says the Lord GOD, "Behold, I am laying in Zion a stone, a tested stone, A costly cornerstone for the foundation, firmly placed. He who believes in it will not be disturbed.*

**(Isaiah 28:16 NASB 1995)**

*They devoted themselves to the apostles'
teaching and to the fellowship, to the breaking of bread and to prayer. Everyone was
filled with awe, and many wonders and miraculous signs were done by the apostles.*

**(Acts 2:42–43 NIV)**

*Trust in the LORD forever, for the LORD, the
LORD, is the Rock eternal.*

**(Isaiah 26:4 NIV)**

# SEEING HIS GOODNESS

To a golfer, winning a vacation at a world-famous golf resort would be a dream come true, but if you did not enjoy the sport at all, you would not take much pleasure in the idea. However, if we happened to know that golf is the passion of the prize winner, we could better understand how they might be elated over the win. We could see the good in it for them. Many times, we judge whether something is good or not according to whether we like it or not. This is not always how God sees things. As you walk through your day, ask God how He sees what is going on. Ask Him to give you His perspective. Pray that you will perceive the goodness of the Lord in your life.

> Father, I realize I do not have Your view of things. You have good plans, and I can trust You, but right not it does not seem so good to me. Help me to have Your perspective. Teach me to rely on You and trust Your ways. In Jesus Name, Amen.

*I remain confident of this: I will see the goodness of the LORD in the land of the living.*

*Wait for the Lord; be strong and take heart
and wait for the LORD.*

**(Psalm 27:13–14 NIV)**

*Because of your great compassion you did
not abandon them in the wilderness. By day
the pillar of cloud did not fail to guide them
on their path, nor the pillar of fire by night to
shine on the way they were to take. You gave
your good Spirit to instruct them. You did not
withhold your manna from their mouths, and
you gave them water for their thirst. For forty
years you sustained them in the wilderness;
they lacked nothing, their clothes did not
wear out nor did their feet become swollen.*

**(Nehemiah 9:19–21 NIV)**

*Consider it pure joy, my brothers and sisters,
whenever you face trials of many kinds, because you know that the testing of your faith
produces perseverance. Let perseverance finish its work so that you may be mature and
complete, not lacking anything. If any of you
lacks wisdom, you should ask God, who gives
generously to all without finding fault, and it
will be given to you.*

**(James 1:2–5 NIV)**

*and pray in my behalf, that speech may be
given to me in the opening of my mouth, to
make known with boldness the mystery of*

*the gospel, for which I am an ambassador in chains; that in proclaiming it I may speak boldly, as I ought to speak.*

**(Ephesians 6:19–20 NASB)**

# STEADFAST MIND

Our minds naturally wander to the "what if" questions, especially when we are tired. Just as in a scary movie, we seem to be able to think of any scenario which would be the worst outcome. Our tendencies to focus on the difficulties become more powerful when we are in situations we cannot control. Thankfully, because we have the truth of Christ to come back to as our plumb line, we can be reminded by God's Word that our hope is in Him, and He is the light who will lead us through the darkness.

Lord Jesus, remind us often that You are our hope and our guide in this valley of shadows where we now seem to be walking. Your presence provides enough light to see each step and gives us peace of mind in the midst of turmoil. Keep us focused on Your truth. You were here in the beginning and are here now. Thank you for being with us. Amen.

*You will keep in perfect peace whose minds are steadfast, because they trust in you.*

**(Isaiah 26:3 NIV)**

*Your word is a lamp for my feet, a light for my path.*

**(Psalm 119:105 NIV)**

*When Jesus spoke again to the people, he said, "I am the light of the world. Whoever follows me will never walk in darkness, but will have the light of life."*

**(John 8:12 NIV)**

*But you are a chosen people, a royal priesthood, a holy nation, God's special possession, that you may declare the praises of him who called you out of darkness and into his wonderful light.*

**(1 Peter 2:9 NIV)**

*In the beginning was the Word, and the Word was with God, and the Word was God. He was with God in the beginning. Through him all things were made; without him nothing was made that has been made. In him was life, and that life was the light of mankind. The light shines in the darkness, and the darkness has not overcame it.*

**(John 1:1–5 NIV)**

# SOUL FOOD

When Paul tells us about being in prison, he said he was exposed to death again and again. He was stoned, shipwrecked, flogged, and more! His physical body was put to the extreme tests, but spiritually and emotionally, he seemed to flourish. Paul realized the keys to survival and to finding joy in the midst of horrific circumstances. His example shows us that we can feed our spirit with the Word of God and with worship and thrive in spite of difficulties. We can feed our body with food, but it is easy to forget that we can nourish our spirit with God's truths, worship, and prayer. Paul encourages us to count our trials joy because they develop Christ-like character in us. Paul tells us that even when his outer self is wasting away, his inner self is being renewed. How did he endure the trials? He knew that it meant he received more grace in the trials, and thus he became more like Christ, which brought all the glory to God.

*"Dear Lord, help us to see Your grace in this season. You are developing more compassion and character in us through these trials. Help us to*

worship and find You in the middle of the adversities. We can trust Your purposes. Thank you for reminding us that we can even flourish in trials. Amen.

*I have worked harder, been in prison more frequently, been flogged more severely, and been exposed to death again and again. Five times I received from the Jews the forty lashes minus one. Three times I was beaten with rods, once I was pelted with stones, three times I was shipwrecked, I spent a night and a day in the open sea, I have been constantly on the move. I have been in danger from rivers, in danger from bandits, in danger from my fellow Jews, in danger from Gentiles; in danger in the city, in danger in the country, in danger at sea; and in danger from false believers. I have labored and toiled and have often gone without sleep; I have known hunger and thirst and have often gone without food; I have been cold and naked. Besides everything else, I face daily the pressure of my concern for all the churches. Who is weak, and I do not feel weak? Who is led into sin, and I do not inwardly burn?*

**(2 Corinthians 11:23b–29 NIV)**

*Be imitators of me, as I am of Christ.*

**(1 Corinthians 11:1 ESV)**

*Consider it pure joy, my brothers and sisters, whenever you face trials of many kinds, because you know that the testing of your faith produces perseverance. Let perseverance finish its work so that you may be mature and complete, not lacking anything. If any of you lacks wisdom, you should ask God, who gives generously to all without finding fault, and it will be given to you.*

**(James 1:2–5 NIV)**

*But we have this treasure in jars of clay to show that this all-surpassing power is from God and not from us. We are hard pressed on every side, but not crushed; perplexed, but not in despair; persecuted, but not abandoned; struck down, but not destroyed. We always carry around in our body the death of Jesus, so that the life of Jesus may also be revealed in our body. For we who are alive are always being given over to death for Jesus' sake, so that his life may also be revealed in our mortal body. So then, death is at work in us, but life is at work in you.*

**(2 Corinthians 4:7–12 NIV)**

*Blessed is the one who perseveres under trial because, having stood the test, that person will receive the crown of life that the Lord has promised to those who love him.*

**(James 1:12 NIV)**

*Therefore we do not lose heart. Though outwardly we are wasting away, yet inwardly we are being renewed day by day. For our light and momentary troubles are achieving for us an eternal glory that far outweighs them all.*

**(2 Corinthians 4:16–17 NIV)**

*Have this mind among yourselves, which is yours in Christ Jesus,*

**(Philippians 2:5 ESV)**

# STABBING PAINS

This caregiving journey is painful at times. You can have hours or days that go so well, and it tricks you into a mindset that says, 'everything is fine.' However, at an unexpected moment, something happens and it feels like someone jabs you in the gut with a sharp knife. It is a frightful jolt reminding us that things are not alright and that our trajectory is heading downward. It seems that just as you begin to heal from the last stabbing, another one injures you. You are walking wounded. And yet, we need to remind ourselves that the Lord is with those who are crushed in spirit. He sees our circumstances. He wants us to talk to Him about how much we are hurting. It may be helpful to read comforting verses from Scripture, to write in a journal, or to talk with someone, in addition to praying.

"Dear Father, we are so tired of hurting. We wonder how long we can continue with these unexpected and repetitive wounds. Take this pain from us and let us know we are not alone. Help us to sense Your presence in our days in the midst of the pain. Help us to focus on You as our loving

Father who has good plans for us and a hope and a future. Things do not look hopeful, but we put our trust in You. Amen.

*The Lord is close to the brokenhearted and saves those who are crushed in spirit.*

**(Psalm 34:18 NIV)**

*He heals the brokenhearted and binds up their wounds.*

**(Psalm 147:3 NIV)**

*When anxiety was great within me, your consolation brought me joy.*

**(Psalm 94:19 NIV)**

*Such things were written in the Scriptures long ago to teach us. And the Scriptures give us hope and encouragement as we wait patiently for God's promises to be fulfilled.*

**(Romans 15:4 NLT)**

*When you pass through the waters, I will be with you; and when you pass through the rivers, they will not sweep over you. When you walk through the fire, you will not be burned; the flames will not set you ablaze.*

**(Isaiah 43:2 NIV)**

*For I know the plans I have for you, declares the Lord, plans to prosper you and not to harm you, plans to give you hope and a future.*

**(Jeremiah 29:11 NIV)**

# IN THEIR SHOES

Even though this journey is one of the most difficult seasons of life, it may be even harder for the loved one we care for today. Can we even imagine what they are going through or what their losses have been recently? It is truly grieving to put ourselves in their shoes. Some may have lost memory, physical abilities, independence, time with family and friends, and more. There may be many areas in their lives where they have become incapacitated to some extent. They may no longer be able to groom themselves or engage fully with others because of hearing loss, fatigue, or illness. They are in the dying process, but they are still alive and realizing what they no longer have. We want to give them the best possible days we can but often feel very helpless. We must remember that God numbers our days, and He knows the whole picture. It may or may not make more sense one day. We have to trust Him and ask for supernatural love, patience, kindness, gentleness and grace. We want to love them well as long as we can. We want to carry the burdens with them.

Dear Father, this is so hard! I don't think there is any way to prepare for this season, but we are in it now. Help us see Your hand in this. Help us give Your love and grace to our loved ones. We want to be Your hands and feet to serve them in this stage of life. We need Your wisdom and the fruits of your Spirit. Amen.

*There is a time for everything, and a season for every activity under the heavens: A time to be born and a time to die, a time to plant and a time to uproot, a time to kill and a time to heal, a time to tear down and a time to build, a time to weep and a time to laugh, a time to mourn and a time to dance, a time to scatter stones and a time to gather them, a time to embrace and a time to refrain from embracing, a time to search and a time to give up, a time to keep and a time to throw away, a time to tear and a time to mend, a time to be silent and a time to speak, a time to love and a time to hate, a time for war and a time for peace.*

**(Ecclesiastes 3:1–8 NIV)**

*But the fruit of the Spirit is love, joy, peace, forbearance, kindness, goodness, faithfulness, gentleness and self-control. Against such things there is no law.*

**(Galatians 5:22–23 NIV)**

*Be completely humble and gentle; be patient, bearing with one another in love.*

**(Ephesians 4:2 NIV)**

*I pray that out of his glorious riches he may strengthen you with power through his Spirit in your inner being, so that Christ may dwell in your hearts through faith. And I pray that you, being rooted and established in love, may have power, together with all the Lord's holy people, to grasp how wide and long and high and deep is the love of Christ,*

**(Ephesians 3:16–18 NIV)**

*Carry each other's burdens, and in this way you will fulfill the law of Christ.*

**(Galatians 6:2 NIV)**

# TIPPING THE SCALE

We experience tough days, but with grace, we keep on going. However, when something is added to our day that might be emotionally disturbing such as a disagreement with a friend or a hard conversation with one of our children, we can feel like this stress tips our scales, and we have trouble dealing with the strain. Our energy is already exhausted, and our emotions are fragile due to the daily trials we face. Watching our loved ones decline strips us of much margin for dealing with emotional issues. But this is real life, and difficult things do happen on a regular basis. How can we find that additional power to make it through these extra difficulties? It has to be supernatural power to carry us through. Our God is supernatural, super powerful, and He tells us to call on Him. Tell Him, yell to Him, ask Him to empower you with His grace.

Dear Lord, we need Your help. We are calling out to You! We have days that are difficult, so we need You to renew our strength because we have nothing left. We can't do this on our own. Hold us up and carry us. Amen.

*But they who wait for the LORD shall renew their strength; they shall mount up with wings like eagles; they shall run and not be weary; they shall walk and not faint.*

**(Isaiah 40:31 ESV)**

*The steps of a man are established by the LORD, when he delights in his way; though he fall, he shall not be cast headlong, for the LORD upholds his hand.*

**(Psalms 37: 23–24 ESV)**

*But truly God has listened; he has attended to the voice of my prayer. Blessed be God, because he has not rejected my prayer or removed his steadfast love from me!*

**(Psalms 66:19–20 ESV)**

*I can do everything through him who gives me strength.*

**(Philippians 4:13 NIV)**

*Be strong and courageous. Do not be afraid or terrified because of them, for the LORD your God goes with you; he will never leave you nor forsake you.*

**(Deuteronomy 31:6 NIV)**

*I call upon the LORD, who is worthy to be praised, and I am saved from my enemies.*

**(2 Samuel 22:4 ESV)**

*In my distress I called upon the LORD, and cried to my God for help; from his temple he heard my voice, and my cry for help before Him, came into His ears.*

**(Psalms 18:6 NIV)**

*As for me, I call to God, and the LORD saves me.*

**(Psalms 55:16 NIV)**

*Call to Me and I will answer you and tell you great and unsearchable things you do not know.*

**(Jeremiah 33:3 NIV)**

# PUT ON A GOOD FACE

So many times during the day, it hits me that I'm losing my loved one bit by bit. It stabs me like an emotional dart to my heart. However, I have to put on a positive face in front of my loved one because I realize that her emotions often play off of mine. I want her to be hopeful, and it is oftentimes advantageous when she is unaware of the heartache in front of us. (I am not talking about being unrealistic in our hope, but having a hopeful attitude.) We have to hold up our loved ones emotionally when possible, but this leaves us grieving in private or containing our grief for the moment. Sometimes this can be unhealthy, so we want to be sure to process these emotions at appropriate times. It may mean waiting until after their bedtime and then getting alone with the Lord and crying out to Him. We also can call friends or family and ask them to hear us out and then to lift our hurts to the Lord. We need Him and others to help us now!

Dear Father, sometimes we don't think we can take the heartache we face. It often comes at us unexpectedly and immediately, and it catches us off guard. Help us to walk in a way that honors our loved ones and honors You. Help us to lay our burdens at Your feet. We trust You and Your timing. Take our grief and give us peace. In Jesus Name, Amen.

*The righteous cry out, and the LORD hears and delivers them out of all their troubles.*

**(Psalm 34:17 ESV)**

*Bear one another's burdens, and so fulfill the law of Christ.*

**(Galatians 6:2 ESV)**

*Humble yourselves, therefore, under God's mighty hand, that he may lift you up in due time. Cast all your anxiety upon him because he cares for you.*

**(1 Peter 5:6–7 NIV)**

*For I am the LORD your God, who takes hold of your right hand and says to you, Do no fear; I will help you.*

**(Isaiah 41:13 NIV)**

*Cast your burden on the LORD, and he will sustain you; he will never permit the righteous to be moved.*

**(Psalm 55:22 ESV)**

*And God is able to make all grace abound to you, so that having all sufficiency in all things at all times, you may abound in every good work.*

**(2 Corinthians 9:8 ESV)**

*For where two or three are gathered in my name, there am I among them.*

**(Matthew 18:20 ESV)**

# CHANGES

There are so many adjustments in this season of life. Changes are different in each circumstance. Often when you begin to care for another, you, in essence, amend roles. You become responsible for many of the decisions regarding their care. If you are now caring for your parent, then it is a dramatic role reversal. We may find ourselves mentally questioning, *Am I really having to discuss this? Is it time for me to take this over? How much longer will they be able to handle this task before it is not possible to continue? Have we made a shift permanently so that they will never be able to do what they did before?* We can find comfort knowing that our God does not change and that He walks with us and guides us through our transitions.

Dear Father, continue to give us the wisdom to make the choices we are faced with in this season. Envelope us with Your Spirit as we face things we have not experienced before. We want to bring You glory in all our ways. Teach us how to do that. Thank you for being a reliable, steadfast God. Amen.

*For I the LORD do not change; therefore you, O children of Jacob, are not consumed.*

**(Malachi 3:6 ESV)**

*Jesus Christ is the same yesterday today and forever.*

**(Hebrews 13:8 NIV)**

*I will instruct you and teach you in the way you should go; I will counsel you with my loving eye on you.*

**(Psalm 32:8 NIV)**

*Trust in the LORD with all your heart. Never rely on what you think you know. Remember the Lord in everything you do, and he will show you the right way.*

**(Proverbs 3:5–6 GNT)**

*The LORD himself goes before you and will be with you; he will never leave you nor forsake you. Do not be afraid; do not be discouraged.*

**(Deuteronomy 31:8 NIV)**

# ONE WAY WINDOW

There are days, sometimes weeks when it feels as if we are not engaged with the real world. We are so occupied with our role as a caregiver that it seems like we are watching everyone else through a one-way window. Their lives move on and change and progress normally, while it feels as if our lives have stood still. Because we are in the midst of this time behind the window, it gives us the impression that no one notices us and that they are going on with their lives while we are merely keeping our head above the water. God sees us and knows where we are and what we are experiencing. He watches all our paths; we have not been forgotten.

Dear Lord, thank you for remembering us all the time, even knowing us before we were born. You know our path, and we submit our ways to You again today. Thank you for being ever faithful. Amen.

*Does He not see my ways and number all my steps?*

**(Job 31:4 ESV)**

*For your ways are in full view of the LORD, and he examines all your paths.*

**(Proverbs 5:21 NIV)**

*The LORD looks down from heaven; he sees all the children of man; from where he sits enthroned he looks out on all the inhabitants of the earth, he who fashions the hearts of them all and observes all their deeds.*

**(Psalm 33:13–15 ESV)**

O LORD, You have searched me and known me! You know when I sit down and when I rise up; you discern my thoughts from afar.

(Psalm 139:1–2 ESV)

*Thereafter, Hagar used another name to refer to the LORD, who had spoken to her. She said, "You are the God who sees me." She also said, "Have I truly seen the One who sees me?*

**(Genesis 16:13 NLT)**

*He will not let your foot slip—he who watches over you will not slumber; (...) The LORD watches over you—the LORD is your shade at your right hand; the sun will not harm you by day, nor the moon by night. The LORD will keep you from all harm—he will watch over your life; the LORD will watch over your coming and going both now and forevermore.*

**(Psalm 121:3, 5–8 NIV)**

# THANKFUL

So many days are difficult, but each day brings something to be thankful for... we simply may have to look a little harder. It sometimes helps to make a journal or a daily list of ideas or happenings so that we become more aware of them. Focus on the little items around you. It could be as simple as being grateful for your cup of coffee that morning or blessed by a pretty sunset, or appreciative for a good phone conversation with a friend. Start paying attention to small joys that God is placing in your path, and they become easier to notice. Once you develop a pattern of naming or listing these, the thankful moments seem to multiply!

Father, help us to be thankful in all situations. Help us to focus on You. We are grateful that Your love never ceases and Your mercies never come to an end. May we be aware of and thankful for the many blessings You put in our days. Amen.

*Rejoice always, pray continually, give thanks in all circumstances; for this is God's will for you in Christ Jesus.*

**(1 Thessalonians 5:16–18 NIV)**

*The steadfast love of the LORD never ceases; his mercies never come to an end; they are new every morning; great is your faithfulness.*

**(Lamentations 3:22–23 ESV)**

*Give thanks to the LORD, for he is good; his love endures forever.*

**(1 Chronicles 16:34 NIV)**

*Devote yourselves to prayer, being watchful and thankful.*

**(Colossians 4:2 NIV)**

*Do not be anxious about anything, but in every situation, by prayer and petition, with thanksgiving, present your requests to God.*

**(Philippians 4:6 NIV)**

*The LORD is my strength and my shield; my heart trusts in him, and he helps me. My heart leaps for joy, and with my song I praise him.*

**(Psalm 28:7 NIV)**

*Therefore, since we are receiving a kingdom that cannot be shaken, let us be thankful, and so worship God acceptably with reverence and awe,*

**(Hebrews 12:28 NIV)**

*And let the peace of Christ rule in your hearts, to which indeed you were called in one body. And be thankful.*

**(Colossians 3:15 ESV)**

# TAKE A LITTLE TIME

Days fold into weeks, and we trudge ahead, not realizing that we are wearing down. It is critical to take some time away from our situation. Just a little break of some sort can be so refreshing. Doing a different activity from your routine can be invigorating. The Lord promises to refresh us, but we are responsible for taking time from our day to seek Him and gather respite. If you have difficulty getting away, consider even going outside if you are always inside and playing music or just listening to the birds and the wind. The Lord has a multitude of ways to restore our soul—just find a little wisp of time!

Lord, you tell us that You refresh our soul. Walk with us and direct us to the refreshing place. Carve out time in our day to seek You and to be restored. Thank You for taking our weariness and giving us strength. Amen.

*The LORD is my shepherd, I lack nothing.*
*He makes me lie down in green pastures, he*
*leads me beside quiet waters, he refreshes my*

*soul. He guides me along the right paths for his name's sake.*

**(Psalm 23:1–3 NIV)**

*You gave abundant showers, O God; you refreshed your weary inheritance.*

**(Psalm 68:9 NIV)**

*I will refresh the weary and satisfy the faint."*

**(Jeremiah 31:25 NIV)**

*The law of the LORD is perfect, refreshing the soul. The statutes of the LORD are trustworthy, making wise the simple.*

**(Psalm 19:7 NIV)**

*Praise be to the God and Father of our Lord Jesus Christ, the Father of compassion and the God of all comfort, who comforts us in all our troubles, so that we can comfort those in any trouble with the comfort we ourselves receive from God.*

**(2 Corinthians 1:3–4 NIV)**

# WHITEOUT

Sometimes we hit a whiteout. We lose perspective of everything. A total snowstorm moves in, and a big snowball or something hits us. We go downhill fast. In this storm, we feel overwhelmed and the things we may have once used accomplished just stop. We try to come out of the blizzard and regain our footing. Too many things at once have fallen off the wheels, and it seems the train wrecked. We try to catch our breath. We hope to see daylight soon. Even when we can't see anything, we hope in Jesus and not in our circumstances. He will hang in there with us even in the storm. Jesus also faced difficult trials. He did not want to be where He was at times, but Jesus looked to the Father for guidance. He cried out and asked if He could give up, if the cup could pass from him, but then submitted to the Father. We can cry out, and when we seek Him, we find Him—our God who suffers with us.

Dear Jesus, we feel lost in the midst of our circumstances. We can't see anything anymore. We need to know You are here with us. We are crying out to You! We don't feel afraid as much as numb, bewildered, and weary. Come and refresh and restore us. Father, we recognize our constant need for You. Come Holy Spirit and fill us. Amen.

The he said to them, "My soul is overwhelmed with sorrow to the point of death. Stay here and keep watch with me." Going a little farther, he fell with his face to the ground and prayed, "My Father, if it is possible, may this cup be taken from me. Yet not as I will, but as you will."

**(Matthew 26:38–39 NIV)**

My God, my God, why have you forsaken me? Why are you so far from saving me, so far from my cries of anguish? My God, I cry out by day, but you do not answer, by night, but I find no rest. Yet you are enthroned as the Holy One; you are the one Israel praises. In you our ancestors put their trust; they trusted and you delivered them. To you they cried out and were saved; in you they trusted and were not put to shame..

**(Psalm 22:1–5 NIV)**

Even though I walk through the darkest valley, I will fear no evil, for you are with me; your rod and your staff, they comfort me.

**(Psalm 23:4 NIV)**

*So we do not lose heart. Though our outer self is wasting away, our inner self is being renewed day by day. For this light momentary affliction is preparing for us an eternal weight of glory beyond all comparison, as we look not to the things that are seen but to the things that are unseen. For the things that are seen are transient, but the things that are unseen are eternal.*

**(2 Corinthians 4:16–18 ESV)**

# PACE YOURSELF

"Pace yourself," this is the advice experts give to runners in a marathon who want to finish well. The problem with this strategy in caregiving for another is that this "race" is comparable to running for two people when you are just one. It also seems almost impossible because our journey has an unknown finish line in regard to time. We can attempt to prepare ahead and have backup plans in place, but the only sure thing we will face is change. So our "pacing" strategy needs to keep looking to the Father whether we are stuck at a standstill or running full blast ahead or even when we have fallen backward. Keep looking to the Father, one step at a time. Pace ourselves.

*"Dear Lord, Help us to keep You in our focus. We are in this race that has no trail markings and no exact finish line. The only way we can run this race day by day is to keep our eyes on You and not the course. Order our steps that we may honor You. Amen.*

*The heart of man plans his way, but the LORD establishes his steps.*

**(Proverbs 16:9 ESV)**

*My steps have held fast to your paths; my feet have not slipped.*

**(Psalm 17:5 ESV)**

*The steps of a man are established by the LORD, when he delights in his way; though he fall, he shall not be cast headlong, for the LORD upholds his hand.*

**(Psalm 37:23–24 ESV)**

*Therefore, since we are surrounded by so great a cloud of witnesses, let us also lay aside every weight, and sin which clings so closely, and let us run with endurance the race that is set before us,*

**(Hebrews 12:1 ESV)**

# DO NOT LOSE HEART

Jesus knew what it was like to lose all his physical abilities on the cross. He looked to the Father for strength to make it through. He trusted God's plan even though circumstances appeared hopeless. Because Jesus was aware of His Father's character and attributes, He could hope in God in spite of his situation. We serve this same God who has unchanging characteristics. That hope is also ours even in this season. Our God is good, trustworthy, reliable, and loving.

> "Lord we seek You for our hope. Remind us again of who You are and how You love us. Teach us to let go of any fear we may have as we look around us and to put our trust in You. You are the God of hope and comfort. We find peace in knowing that You never change. Amen.

*Jesus Christ is the same yesterday and today and forever.*

**(Hebrews 13:8 ESV)**

*For I the LORD do not change; therefore you,
O children of Jacob, are not consumed.*

**(Malachi 3:6 ESV)**

*Have you not known? Have you not heard?
The LORD is the everlasting God, the Creator
of the ends of the earth. He does not faint or
grow weary; his understanding is unsearchable.*

**(Isaiah 40:28 ESV)**

*We remember before our God and Father your
work produced by faith, your labor prompted
by love, and your endurance inspired by hope
in our Lord Jesus Christ.*

**(1 Thessalonians 1:3 NIV)**

*Oh, taste and see that the LORD is good!
Blessed is the man who takes refuge in him!*

**(Psalm 34:8 ESV)**

*Every good gift and every perfect gift is from
above, coming down from the Father of lights
with whom there is no variation or shadow
due to change.*

**(James 1:17 ESV)**

# SECRET PLACE

Sometimes we just need to hide and get away from all the demands in our lives. We yearn to go to the secret place with Jesus and get replenished. Our soul seems weary and needs refreshment. We need to remember that the Holy Spirit is our intercessor, comforter, and counselor. We can go to Him and seek restoration. He will sustain us. He will lift our heads. We can call out to the Holy Spirit, and He will come to our aid.

*Holy Spirit, thank you for being our paraclete. We are so grateful that we can call on the Holy Spirit to be our dependable sustainer. May we have time today to seek Your presence and to know Your comfort. Amen.*

*How lovely is your dwelling place, LORD Almighty! My soul yearns, even faints, for the courts of the Lord; my heart and my flesh cry out for the living God.*

**(Psalm 84:1–2 NIV)**

*Yes, my soul, find rest in God; my hope comes from him. Truly he is my rock and my salvation; he is my fortress, I will not be shaken. My salvation and my honor depend on God; he is my mighty rock, my refuge. Trust in Him at all times, you people; pour out your hearts to him, for God is our refuge.*

**(Psalm 62:5–8 NIV)**

*But when the Helper comes, whom I will sent to you from the Father, the Spirit of truth, who proceeds from the Father, he will bear witness about me.*

**(John 15:26 ESV)**

*Praise be to the God and Father of our Lord Jesus Christ, the Father of compassion and the God of all comfort, who comforts us in all our troubles, so that we can comfort those in any trouble with the comfort we ourselves receive from God.*

**(2 Corinthians 1:3–4 NIV)**

# YOU HOLD US

We sometimes feel like we are alone like no one can understand what we are walking through on a daily basis. Many days we could not describe to someone else what has happened since it is so unbelievable even to us. Because of Your Word we know that the truth is we are not alone. No matter what we are experiencing, You are with us in it. Just as on a sailboat, most see the sail and notice how the wind catches it to move the boat. But the key part of the sail is the strong mast that holds it up. It is the key ingredient to keeping the sail up. You are the mast to hold us. We are so grateful for Your strength and your stability in our lives.

Dear Father, thank you for holding us up and being the stability in our lives. We recognize our dependence on You. We need You in our lives now and forever. Amen.

*So do not fear, for I am with you; do not be dismayed, for I am your God. I will strengthen you and help you; I will uphold you with my righteous right hand.*

**(Isaiah 41:10 NIV)**

163

*The LORD upholds all those who fall and lifts up all who are bowed down.*

**(Psalm 145:14 NIV)**

*But you, Lord, are a shield around me, my glory, the One who lifts my head high.*

**(Psalm 3:3 NIV)**

*I am still confident of this: I will see the goodness of the LORD in the land of the living. Wait for the LORD; be strong and take heart and wait for the LORD.*

**(Psalm 27:13–14 NIV)**

# GREATER PURPOSE

We may have pictured ourselves as being created for a specific task or area. Many times we define ourselves by our roles or job descriptions. Becoming a caregiver often changes our lives and especially the ways we are able to spend our time. We may have defined ourselves in a certain way before we began caregiving, but God always saw us as His child and that definition has not changed. Our identity in Christ remains the same. We can ask Him what His vision is for our lives. Be open to what He wants to do with you in this season. For example, did you know that play dough was invented to clean soot off walls? Once vinyl wallpaper was created, this formula became obsolete, so it was remarketed as a fun clay for children! Let's ask ourselves, is there something new God is doing with us in this season?

Father, we start with our vision and our purposes, but what we really want is Your purpose for our lives. We often try to take control of our lives and forget to listen to You. Please forgive us. Give us Your vision for our lives in this season. Show us Your purpose in these days. Amen.

*The Lord will vindicate me; your love, Lord, endures forever— do not abandon the works of your hands.*

**(Psalm 138:8 NIV)**

*I thank my God every time I remember you. In all my prayers for all of you, I always pray with joy because of your partnership in the gospel from the first day until now, being confident of this, that he who began a good work in you will carry it on to completion until the day of Christ Jesus.*

**(Philippians 1:3–6 NIV)**

*For if you remain silent at this time, liberation and rescue will arise for the Jews from another place, and you and your father's house will perish [since you did not help when you had the chance]. And who knows whether you have attained royalty for such a time as this [and for this very purpose].*

**(Esther 4:14 AMP)**

*But the plans of the LORD stand firm forever, the purposes of his heart through all generations.*

**(Psalm 33:11 NIV)**

*But do not forget this one thing, dear friends; With the Lord a day is like a thousand years, and a thousand years are like a day.*

**(2 Peter 3:8 NIV)**

*There is a time for everything, and a season
for every activity under the heavens:*

**(Ecclesiastes 3:1 NIV)**

# DESERT INVITATIONS

We need to realize that sometimes God uses a desert experience to bring us closer to Him. The desert may be an invitation to intimacy with Him. He can fulfill us even in our seasons of lack. We may view our situation as desolate and unproductive. These circumstances are an opportunity to see His faithfulness and kindness. Spend time with God today, asking Him what He has for you in this place.

Dear Lord, we trust Your ways even though in our view this all looks rather hopeless. Father, what do You want to teach me in this time? What do You have for me as I walk in this desolate place? I know You have good for me, so I declare that now. In Jesus Name, Amen.

*Therefore I am now going to allure her; I will lead her into the wilderness and speak tenderly to her. There will I give her back her vineyards, and will make the Valley of Achor a door of hope. There she will respond as in the days of her youth, as in the day she came up out of Egypt.*

**(Hosea 2:14–15 NIV)**

*As for God, his way is perfect: The Lord's word is flawless; he shields all who take refuge in him.*

**(Psalm 18:30 NIV)**

*Yet you, LORD, are our Father. We are the clay, you are the potter; we are all the work of your hand.*

**(Isaiah 64:8 NIV)**

*I cared for you in the wilderness, in the land of burning heat.*

**(Hosea 13:5 NIV)**

*For the LORD your God has blessed you in all the work of your hands. He knows your going through this great wilderness. These forty years the LORD your God has been with you. You have lacked nothing.*

**(Deuteronomy 2:7 ESV)**

# NO RUSH

It is difficult to remember that His timing is perfect. We cannot rush complicated and exhausting seasons. God can do whatever He wants in a short time or a longer duration. His plan is so intricate, and we may never know why things happen the way they do. We tend to think we know how everything should best work out in the days or weeks or years, but reality is that we have to let go of our expectations and trust His plan.

When we know His character, we can trust His timing.

Father, we want to hurry through some of this desert season. We want everything to be better now. Help us to rest in Your timing and to trust in Your ways. Amen.

*But do not forget one thing, my dear friends! There is no difference in the Lord's sight between one day and a thousand years; to him the two are the same.*

**(2 Peter 3:8 GNT)**

171

*You may make your plans, but God directs your actions.*

**(Proverbs 16:9 GNT)**

*The LORD is good to those who wait for him, to the soul who seeks him.*

**(Lamentations 3:25 ESV)**

*For the revelation awaits an appointed time; it speaks of the end and will not prove false. Though it linger, wait for it; it will certainly come and will not delay.*

**(Habakkuk 2:3 NIV)**

*Wait for the LORD; be strong, and let your heart take courage; wait for the LORD!*

**(Psalm 27:14 ESV)**

*And let us not grow weary of doing good, for in due season we will reap, if we do not give up.*

**(Galatians 6:9 ESV)**

*He said to them, "It is not for you to know times or seasons that the Father has fixed by his own authority."*

**(Acts 1:7 ESV)**

# PRAYER IS OUR WEAPON

Sometimes we feel helpless, and it seems we have no power to change anything. However, the Bible specifically tells us that prayer is our weapon to fight battles. God instructs us to be persistent and have a humble attitude when we come to Him. It is empowering to know that we can be actively fighting the enemy and petitioning the heavens for help through our prayers. Our Father did not leave us defenseless in this battle! He has equipped us!

Father, thank you for listening to our prayers. Thank you for equipping us in this battle. Help us to be persistent and not give up. We understand that Your timing is perfect, and we must rest in that. Remind us to lay our burdens at Your feet and to expect Your Holy Spirit to counsel and comfort us. Amen.

*The weapons we fight with are not the weapons of the world. On the contrary, they have divine power to demolish strongholds. We demolish arguments and every pretension that sets itself up against the knowledge of God, and we take captive every thought to make it obedient to Christ.*

**(2 Corinthians 10:4–5 NIV)**

*Finally, be strong in the Lord and in the strength of his might. Put on the whole armor of God, that you may be able to stand against the schemes of the devil (...) praying at all times in the Spirit, with all prayer and supplication. To that end, keep alert with all perseverance, making supplication for all the saints.*

**(Ephesians 6:10, 11, 18 ESV)**

*Therefore confess your sins to each other and pray for each other so that you may be healed. The prayer of a righteous person is powerful and effective.*

**(James 5:16 NIV)**

*I face your holy Temple, bow down, and praise your name because of your constant love and faithfulness, because you have shown that your name and your commands are supreme.*

**(Psalms 138:2 GNT)**

*Humble yourselves, then, under God's mighty hand, so that he will lift you up in his own good time. Leave all your worries with him, because he cares for you.*

**(1 Peter 5:6–7 GNT)**

# RELY ON HIM

Thriving in this season is not about how perfect we accomplish our task at hand or how much we try. In accepting Christ as our Lord, we have already admitted that we cannot do this on our own, and we do not want to walk this life without Him. His amazing Holy Spirit brings us wisdom, comfort, and counsel. His truth is our solid foundation that anchors us in the storms. His Father's love for us is reliable. He will never abandon us.

Dear Father, it is difficult for us to trust fully in You. We get used to completing tasks and hurrying about our days without even consulting You. Forgive us because we do need and want You. Help us to learn to rely on You in all our ways. You are such a loving Father and amazing God who is worthy to be trusted. Teach us to seek You continually and to stand on Your Word. Amen.

*"Am I a God nearby," declares the LORD, "And not a God far away? Who can hide in secret places so that I cannot see them?" de-*

175

clares the LORD. *"Do not I fill heaven and earth?" declares the LORD.*

**(Jeremiah 23:23–24 NIV)**

*Be strong and courageous. Do not be afraid or terrified because of them, for the LORD your God goes with you; he will never leave you nor forsake you."*

**(Deuteronomy 31:6 NIV)**

*But seek his kingdom, and these things will be given you as well. "Do not be afraid, little flock, for your Father has been pleased to give you the kingdom.*

**(Luke 12:31–32 NIV)**

*For I, the LORD your God, hold your right hand; it is I who say to you, "Fear not, I am the one who helps you.*

**(Isaiah 41:13 ESV)**

*The LORD is my rock and my fortress and my deliverer, my God, my rock, in whom I take refuge, my shield, and the horn of my salvation, my stronghold.*

**(Psalm 18:2 ESV)**

*Then he said to me, "This is the word of the LORD to Zerubbabel: Not by might, nor by power, but by my Spirit, says the LORD of hosts.*

**(Zechariah 4:6 ESV)**

*Seek the LORD and his strength; seek his presence continually!*

**(1 Chronicles 16:11 ESV)**

*Be strong and courageous. Do not fear or be in dread of them, for it is the LORD your God who goes with you. He will not leave you or forsake you.*

**(Deuteronomy 31:6 ESV)**

*Indeed, we felt that we had received the sentence of death. But that was to make us rely not on ourselves but on God who raises the dead.*

**(2 Corinthians 1:9 ESV)**

# ALWAYS LISTENING

Sometimes we get so caught up in trying to get our daily task list completed that we forget to sit and truly listen to our loved ones. Taking time to listen with our whole self shows them honor, value, and love. It is amazing to recall that our heavenly Father is always available to listen to us. He cares about how we are doing emotionally, what we are dreaming for our lives, and what disappointments we may be facing. He is an example for us to follow as we care for our loved ones.

Dear Father, help us to stop and listen to our loved ones. Remind us to slow the pace and to take time to understand what they may need emotionally. You are such a beautiful example of a father who has time for us, no matter what we are going through or how busy life gets. May we be the hands, feet, and ears of Christ to our loved one. Amen.

*When he had washed their feet and put on his outer garments and resumed his place, he said to them, "Do you understand what I have done to you? You call me Teacher and Lord, and you are right, for so I am. If I then, your Lord and Teacher, have washed your feet, you also ought to wash on another's feet.*

**(John 13:12–14 ESV)**

*By this all people will know that you are my disciples, if you have love for one another."*

**(John 13:35 ESV)**

*When God's people are in need, be ready to help them. Always be eager to practice hospitality.*

**(Romans 12:13 NLT)**

*The eyes of the LORD are on the righteous, and his ears are attentive to their cry;*

**(Psalm 34:15 NIV)**

*let the wise listen and add to their learning, and let the discerning get guidance—*

**(Proverbs 1:5 NIV)**

*A person's thoughts are like water in a deep well, but someone with insight can draw them out.*

**(Proverbs 20:5 GNT)**

*My dear brothers and sisters, take note of this: Everyone should be quick to listen, slow to speak and slow to become angry,*

**(James 1:19 NIV)**

*Hear, O my people, while I admonish you! O Israel, if you would listen to me!*

**(Psalm 81:8 ESV)**

# WHAT IS GOD CALLING ME?

During these days, we may not see ourselves as who God calls us to be. We judge ourselves by outward appearance, standards, and accomplishments. God sees us as His child and as His workmanship. We are the temple of His Holy Spirit! Think about this, do we see an acorn as an oak tree? The acorn is the first developmental stage of a mighty oak. So, if our lives do not look now as we think they should, let us remember the tiny acorn, which one day will be a beautiful and majestic oak tree.

Dear Lord, in these days, we may only be able to see ourselves as a small acorn. We may feel as if we have an unremarkable identity. However, You see us as Your beloved child, and we can rest in that identity. Help us to remember that You created us and have placed Your anointed Holy Spirit in us to equip us for every good work. Amen.

*But the LORD said to Samuel, "Do not look on his appearance or on the height of his stature, because I have rejected him. For the*

*LORD sees not as man sees: man looks on the outward appearance, but the LORD looks on the heart."*

**(1 Samuel 16:7 ESV)**

*Do you not know that you are God's temple and that God's Spirit dwells in you?*

**(1 Corinthians 3:16 ESV)**

*For we are his workmanship, created in Christ Jesus for good works, which God prepared beforehand, that we should walk in them.*

**(Ephesians 2:10 ESV)**

*I pray that out of his glorious riches he may strengthen you with power through his Spirit in your inner being, so that Christ may dwell in your hearts through faith. And I pray that you, being rooted and established in love, may have power, together with all the Lord's hold people, to grasp how wide and long and high and deep is the love of Christ, and to know this love that surpasses knowledge— that you may be filled to the measure of all the fullness of God.*

**(Ephesians 3:16–19 NIV)**

# DAILY GRACE

God gives us grace for today, a grace for what is right in front of us. Day by day, He renews us and supplies us. He does not give grace according to what we deserve, thankfully, but because He desires for us to have it. It is a free gift for those who believe in Him. We can handle whatever comes up today because we can walk in His love and mercy. We do not have to earn this gift, nor do we necessarily deserve it. He is a good Father and gives us better than we deserve. We can face today with that grace!

*Dear Father, thank you for Your amazing grace. You go above and beyond what we could think or imagine in caring for us. May we share that grace with those we love. May we remember that for today, You will provide us with enough grace for all we need. Amen.*

*Therefore do not worry about tomorrow, for tomorrow will worry about itself. Each day has enough trouble of its own.*

**(Matthew 6:34 NIV)**

*Grace and peace be yours in abundance through the knowledge of God and of Jesus our Lord.*

**(2 Peter 1:2 NIV)**

*But to each one of us grace has been given as Christ apportioned it.*

**(Ephesians 4:7 NIV)**

*But his answer was: "My grace is all you need, for my power is greatest when you are weak." I am most happy, then, to be proud of my weaknesses, in order to feel the protection of Christ's power over me.*

**(2 Corinthians 12:9 GNT)**

*And God is able to make all grace abound to you, so that having all sufficiency in all things at all times, you may abound in every good work.*

**(2 Corinthians 9:8 ESV)**

*It is because of the LORD'S lovingkindnesses that we are not consumed, Because His [tender] compassions never fail. They are new every morning; Great and beyond measure is Your faithfulness.*

**(Lamentations 3:22–23 AMP )**

# NEED FOR GOD

In the sermon on the mount, Jesus tells us that those who are "poor in spirit" are blessed. The meaning of blessed could be feeling content and hopeful, even joyful, regardless of our circumstances. Poor in spirit seems to be a phrase describing people who know they are in poverty spiritually without God. As caregivers, we realize that we cannot control the circumstances in this journey, there is no seen justice in where we are, and we have nothing without Christ in us. This season potentially can bring us to the raw awareness that we do not have any power on our own to make things turn out the way we thought they should. We have to lay our expectations at the feet of Jesus, admit we cannot do this on our own, and ask Him to be King of our lives. We need Him. He is the one who can give us hope and joy in spite of our life situation.

Dear Father, teach us to look to You for our hope and joy. May we continue to let go of the idea that we can fix things and that we can handle things and to get to the place where we can give up our independence and submit to You. You are the King, and we are nothing without You. We need You. Thank You for always being ready to receive us. Amen.

*Blessed are the poor in spirit, for theirs is the kingdom of heaven.*

**(Matthew 5:3 NIV)**

*But as for me, I am poor and needy; may the Lord think of me. You are my help and my deliverer; you are my God, do not delay.*

**(Psalm 40:17 NIV)**

*But may all who seek you rejoice and be glad in you; may those who long for your saving help always say, "The Lord is great!" But as for me, I am poor and needy; come quickly to me, O God. You are my help and my deliverer; Lord, do not delay.*

**(Psalm 70:4–5 NIV)**

*And Jesus went with them. When he was not far from the house, the centurion sent friends, saying to him, "Lord, do not trouble yourself, for I am not worthy to have you come under my roof.*

**(Luke 7:6 ESV)**

*And now, God, I'm left with one conclusion: my only hope is to hope in you alone!*

**(Psalm 39:7 TPT)**

# THEY ARE WATCHING

Whether we like it or not, it is reality that other people are watching how we handle this caregiving season. It may be our children, family, neighbors, or even the health care workers we encounter. We have to keep realigning our goal with that of a Believer in Christ. We want to honor Him in all we do. We want to walk like Him, talk like Him, and even be His fragrance to others. This is impossible unless we are living with the power of God's Spirit inside of us. We are only human, but God is supernatural!

Dear Lord, this is such a difficult road to travel. We cannot do this on our own power. We need Your amazing Holy Spirit to equip us and enable us. Help us to be an example of love in action to those who may be watching. Amen.

*Practice these things, immerse yourself in them, so that all may see your progress. Keep a close watch on yourself and on the teaching. Persist in this, for by so doing you will save both yourself and your hearers.*

**(1 Timothy 4:15–16 ESV)**

*For we are to God the pleasing aroma of Christ among those who are being saved and those who are perishing.*

**(2 Corinthians 2:15 NIV)**

*Not that we are sufficient in ourselves to claim anything as coming from us, but our sufficiency is from God,*

**(2 Corinthians 3:5 ESV)**

*Therefore, I urge you, brothers and sisters, in view of God's mercy, to offer your bodies as a living sacrifice, holy and pleasing to God—this is your true and proper worship.*

**(Romans 12:1 NIV)**

# DISPLAYING OUR VALUES

Being a caregiver requires us to consider the needs of others and be willing to respond. Christ models this in many examples in the New Testament. He healed the sick, gave sight to the blind, touched the lepers, and showed compassion to those who were ignored by others. In 1 Timothy, Paul writes of an important principle of taking care of your family. Because our manner of living reveals what is important to us, we actually display our values by our daily lives. As we compassionately care for others, we are conveying the outward message that we are serving and following Christ. We are called to love others as He has loved us and to look to the interests of others. This is what it's like to be a caregiver.

Dear Jesus, help us to remember that You taught us to lay down our lives for others. Continue to develop in us the ability to honor those in our lives. Empower us by Your Holy Spirit to love, honor, and serve even when we don't have the energy or ability on our own to walk this out. Thank you for teaching and equipping us for every season. Amen.

*Anyone who does not provide for their relatives, and especially for their own household, has denied the faith and is worse than an unbeliever.*

**(1 Timothy 5:8 NIV)**

*Do nothing from selfish ambition or conceit, but in humility count others more significant than yourselves. Let each of you look not only to his own interests, but also to the interests of others.*

**(Philippians 2:3–4 ESV)**

*Beloved, let us love one another, for love is from God, and whoever loves has been born of God and knows God. Anyone who does not love does not know God, because God is love.*

**(1 John 4:7–8 ESV)**

*This is my commandment, that you love one another as I have loved you.*

**(John 15:12 ESV)**

*Love one another in brotherly affection. Outdo one another in showing honor.*

**(Romans 12:10 ESV)**

*Greater love has no one than this, that someone lay down his life for his friends.*

**(John 15:13 ESV)**

# HOPE INFUSERS

We all need hope! Encouragement from other people can bring us hope and strength to continue our journey. But what about those times when we have no one to infuse hope to us? Maybe we need to remind ourselves that our family and friends also may be dealing with their struggles. These days, most people have super busy lives with pressures from a variety of sources. If we have not heard in a long while from a certain person who had once been close to us, maybe it is time to send them a note of encouragement. Our wellspring of hope comes from Jesus, so we will always have hope to share with others. We can be the hope infusers!

> Dear Father, may we see people through Your eyes and with Your discernment know how to reach out to them. May we never forget that You are the source of our hope and Your supply is never-ending. Thank You for always having hope available to us. Amen.

*To them God chose to make known how great among the Gentiles are the riches of the glory of this mystery, which is Christ in you, the hope of glory.*

**(Colossians 1:27 ESV)**

*We have this as a sure and steadfast anchor of the soul, a hope that enters into the inner place behind the curtain, where Jesus has gone as a forerunner on our behalf, having become a high priest forever after the order of Melchizedek.*

**(Hebrews 6:19–20 ESV)**

*I pray that the eyes of your heart may be enlightened in order that you may know the hope to which he has called you, the riches of his glorious inheritance in his holy people,*

**(Ephesians 1:18 NIV)**

*You will be secure, because there is hope; you will look about you and take your rest in safety.*

**(Job 11:18 NIV)**

*The LORD is all I have, and so I put my hope in him.*

**(Lamentations 3:24 GNT)**

*Blessed be the God and Father of our Lord Jesus Christ! According to his great mercy, he has caused us to be born again to a living hope through the resurrection of Jesus Christ from the dead, to an inheritance that is imperishable, undefiled, and unfading, kept in heaven for you, who by God's power are being guarded through faith for a salvation ready to be revealed in the last time.*

**(1 Peter 1:3–5 ESV)**

# STOP AND SPEND TIME

Many days are full of chores and duties that directly relate to caring for our loved ones. It is easy to spend time handling all the tasks which seem to make their lives better but not to stop and just be present with our loved ones. It is difficult to remember to do this even though it sounds like common sense. Maybe we could even set a timer or set an appointment time that reminds us to stop all the chores and just soak in time with them. There may be a show that our loved ones like to watch and would enjoy our company when watching. Or they may want to sit on the back porch and watch for the birds, and we can easily join them. Let's get in the habit of taking a time-out from the necessities and enjoying that time with our loved ones. Isn't this what our Heavenly Father desires of us—attentive time with Him?

Dear Father, we admit that we get caught up in crossing off our to-do list of chores required for this role. Help us to stop and pay attention to our loved ones in ways that would honor them. Remind us to focus on them and what their desires may be. We need Your Holy Spirit in this. May we also have steadfast time with You, our heavenly Father. Amen.

*One who has unreliable friends soon comes to ruin, but there is a friend who sticks closer than a brother.*

**(Proverbs 18:24 NIV)**

*Two are better off than one, because together they can work more effectively.*

**(Ecclesiastes 4:9 GNT)**

*Then you will call upon me and come and pray to me, and I will listen to you. You will seek me and find me when you seek me with all your heart.*

**(Jeremiah 29:12–13 NIV)**

*Let love be genuine. Abhor what is evil; hold fast to what is good. Love one another with brotherly affection. Outdo one another in showing honor. Do not be slothful in zeal, be fervent in spirit, serve the Lord. Rejoice in hope, be patient in tribulation, be constant in prayer. Contribute to the needs of the saints and seek to show hospitality.*

**(Romans 12:9–13 ESV)**

*So then, as we have the opportunity, let us do good to everyone, and especially to those who are of the household of faith.*

**(Galatians 6:10 ESV)**

# DUAL ROLES

There are many instances where we serve two (or more) roles in our lives. For example, an airline pilot could also be a mother and a wife. However, usually, she would not have her husband and children on the plane she is flying and be expected to parent her children as she flies the airplane. But that is oftentimes what we are expected to do as caregivers. We are to be a caregiver while at the same time we are trying to fulfill other roles such as a parent, spouse, employee, etc. It can become difficult to balance all the roles and to feel like we are doing justice to any of them. It is important to give ourselves some grace in this season. Talk to the others in your life who may be indirectly involved in this caregiving experience and let them know you realize that they may be encountering changes in the relationship. Share your thoughts and your feelings with them and allow them to step in to be a part of changes for the better.

*Dear Lord, sometimes it feels like we fall short in all areas because there is so much expected of us. Help us to verbalize our situations to those in*

our lives who are important to us. Help us to understand that You design us as a body of Christ
so that we can have each other to help along the
way. Teach us to have grace for ourselves along
the way. Amen.

*Rejoice with those who rejoice, weep with
those who weep.*

**(Romans 12:15 ESV)**

*And he arose and came to his father. But while
he was still a long way off, his father saw him
and felt compassion, and ran and embraced
him and kissed him.*

**(Luke 15:20 ESV)**

*You are so rich in all you have: in faith,
speech, and knowledge, in your eagerness to
help and in your love for us. And so we want
you to be generous also in this service of love.*

**(2 Corinthians 8:7 GNT)**

*The command that Christ has given us is this:
all who love God must love their brother or
sister also.*

**(1 John 4:21 GNT)**

# GIVE THEM INDEPENDENCE

Everyone needs some moments of freedom in their lives. The loved ones we care for probably desire to maintain some segment of their life that can remind them of past normalcy. It is here that we may be able to help them. Seek out and find even the smallest thing that you can continue to facilitate so that your loved one is able to do what they once did before. For example, if they cannot remember how to use the phone, then you can call their friend for them and put the phone on speaker and enable them to have their conversation. Or if they would like to pick out their clothes and it is difficult, then you can tell them what is available and bring them what they choose. It is a process of change because we do not do things the way we used to, but we can alter details and find a way to honor our loved ones by gifting them with a sense of independence.

Dear Father, we want to honor others. Sometimes we do not even realize how this could look in our lives. Help us to see this situation the way You see it and to have the wisdom and discernment to develop new alternatives to the old way of doing things. We know it is sad for our loved ones to have to give up their independence, and we want to carry this burden with them as lovingly as possible. Amen.

Love each other with genuine affection, and take delight in honoring each other.

(Romans 12:10 NLT)

Do nothing from selfish ambition or conceit, but in humility count others more significant than yourselves. Let each of you look not only to his own interests, but also to the interests of others.

(Philippians 2:3–4 ESV)

Honor everyone. Love the brotherhood. Fear God. Honor the emperor.

(1 Peter 2:17 ESV)

Bear one another's burdens, and so fulfill the law of Christ.

(Galatians 6:2 ESV)

For we are taking pains to do what is right, not only in the eyes of the Lord but also in the eyes of man.

(2 Corinthians 8:21 NIV)

If any of you lacks wisdom, you should ask God, who gives generously to all without finding fault, and it will be given to you.

(James 1:5 NIV)

# BE PERFECT?

There is a Scripture that can be overwhelming because it says for us to be perfect as our heavenly Father is perfect. We know that no one can actually be perfect except Jesus, and there is the blessed fact that because of Christ in us, we then can be perfect in God's eyes. However, practically Christ is always calling us to surrender our personal rights for the sake of others. He calls us daily to lay down our lives and be more like Him. As a caregiver, we are walking out what God has created us to do when loving God and loving others sacrificially. This whole journey itself creates in us a more Christlike character. It is a path we are all on to run the race well and to one day be like Him. We will not be perfect today, but every day as we submit to Him and give our lives in love, we become more like Him.

Dear Jesus, we want to be like You. We fail every day in some way, but we again lay our lives down and submit to You. We choose to live out what You are calling us to in this caregiving season. We give our lives for others. May we run this race well. Amen.

*Be perfect, therefore, as your heavenly Father is perfect.*

**(Matthew 5:48 NIV)**

*whoever says he abides in him ought to walk in the same way in which he walked.*

**(1 John 2:6 ESV)**

*For to this you have been called, because Christ also suffered for you, leaving you an example, so that you might follow in his steps.*

**(1 Peter 2:21 ESV)**

*Be imitators of me, as I am of Christ.*

**(1 Corinthians 11:1 ESV)**

*Therefore be imitators of God, as beloved children. And walk in love, as Christ loved us and gave himself up for us, a fragrant offering and sacrifice to God.*

**(Ephesians 5:1–2 ESV)**

*And we all, with unveiled face, beholding the glory of the Lord, are being transformed into the same image from one degree of glory to another. For this comes from the Lord who is the Spirit.*

**(2 Corinthians 3:18 ESV)**

*For we are his workmanship, created in Christ Jesus for good works, which God prepared beforehand, that we should walk in them.*

**(Ephesians 2:10 ESV)**

*Do you not know that in a race all the runners run, but only one gets the prize? Run in such a way as to get the prize.*

**(1 Corinthians 9:24 NIV)**

# SUREFOOTED

Caregiving could be compared to traveling an expedition with an unknown destination and treacherous and unpredictable terrain. We do not know the time this trip will take, nor can we predict the new situations that may arise day by day. Some situations we face are very tricky, and we do not have the expertise or experience to navigate the challenges. Each phase requires a new assessment as to how to negotiate our next steps. It is easy to feel as if we are not equipped or prepared for this season. But God has fitted us with all we need because He walks with us. We can always escape to Him. Just as He created a deer to stand in high places and rocky ledges without slipping, He has equipped us with His Presence.

Lord, sometimes we wonder if we are able to do what is required of us. We don't feel prepared to walk this out and to be the best caregiver. And yet we know that You are our provider, and You give us all we need. You knew ahead of time how this would look, and You equipped us. Help us keep our focus on You. Amen.

*The Sovereign LORD give me strength. He makes me sure-footed as a deer, and keeps me safe on the mountains.*

**(Habakkuk 3:19 GNT)**

*He makes my feet like hind's feet [able to stand firmly and tread safely on paths of testing and trouble]; He sets me [securely] upon my high places.*

**(Psalm 18:33 AMP)**

*It is God who arms me with strength and keeps my way secure. He makes my feet like the feet of a deer; he causes me to stand on the heights. He trains by hands for battle; my arms can bend a bow of bronze. You make your saving help my shield; your help has made me great. You provide a broad path for my feet, so that my ankles do not give way.*

**(2 Samuel 22:33–37 NIV)**

*I will strengthen them in the LORD and in his name they will live securely," declares the LORD.*

**(Zechariah 10:12 NIV)**

*[we pray that you may be] strengthened and invigorated with all power, according to His glorious might, to attain every kind of endurance and patience with joy;*

**(Colossians 1:11 AMP)**

# DECLARING GOD'S BEST

As caregivers, we may be somewhat like a thermostat for an air conditioner. We can set the temperature or the tone by our attitudes and what comes from our mouths. We can declare God's truths out loud so that our loved one can be encouraged in spite of the struggles they face. There is a lot of power in our words. Our mindset and the words we say can bring hope or deliver despair. The Bible has a lot to say about the power of our words. God is our source, so we can go to Him for help in realigning our heart and mind to His way of viewing things. The Holy Spirit can counsel us on our attitude and bring to mind Scriptures to create in us the mind of Christ.

> Father, teach us to declare Your Word over our loved ones. May we be the fragrance of Christ to them and to anyone we meet today. Bathe our minds in Your truths so that we don't get swayed by the difficulties in front of us. May our words carry rivers of living water to those who thirst. Amen.

*He who believes in Me [who adheres to, trusts in, and relies on Me], as the Scripture has said, 'From his innermost being will flow continually rivers of living water.'"*

**(John 7:38 AMP)**

*Keep your heart with all vigilance, for from it flow the springs of life. Put away from you crooked speech, and put devious talk far from you.*

**(Proverbs 4:23–24 ESV)**

*A good man brings good things out of the good stored up in his heart, and an evil man brings evil things out of the evil stored up in his heart. For the mouth speaks what the heart is full of.*

**(Luke 6:45 NIV)**

*"Now yield and submit yourself to Him [agree with God and be conformed to His will] and be at peace; In this way [you will prosper and great] good will come to you. "Please receive the law and instruction from His mouth And establish His words in your heart and keep them.*

**(Job 22:21–22 AMP)**

*When people are brought low and you say, 'Lift them up!' then he will save the downcast.*

**(Job 22:29 NIV)**

# DON'T WASTE ANYTHING

Suffering brings intimacy. God can bring richness out of our trials. Paul, the apostle, is a great example. His arrest in Jerusalem had been unjustified and life-threatening. His imprisonment in Caesarea was underserved. Then he endured many hardships on his travels to Rome, only then to be imprisoned for two years. Paul was imprisoned when he wrote the letters to the Colossians, Philemon, Ephesians, and Philippians. It is obvious that Paul endured much suffering, but he was able to hold on to the belief that God would be honored in them and the gospel would be furthered. During these years, Paul also received visions and interpretations from the Lord. He was able to heal the sick on the island of Malta and survived a poisonous snake bite. His walk with the Lord only grew richer and deeper through his sufferings. That is our hope that in this season of caregiving our relationship with Christ will grow in intimacy.

> *Dear Jesus, we do not want any lessons wasted in this life. May we trust You and, with open arms, be willing to walk fully this sea-*

son of suffering with our loved one no matter what comes our way. May we hear Your voice and be a part of Your miraculous. Change us and allow us to grow more deeply connected to You. Amen." And now, behold, I am going to Jerusalem, constrained by the Spirit, not knowing what will happen to me there, except that the Holy Spirit testifies to me in every city that imprisonment and afflictions await me. But I do not account my life of any value nor as precious to myself, if only I may finish my course and the ministry that I received from the Lord Jesus, to testify to the gospel of the grace of God... And there was much weeping on the part of all; they embraced Paul and kissed him, being sorrowful most of all because of the word he had spoken, that they would not see his face again. And they accompanied him to the ship.

**(Acts 20:22–24, 37–38 ESV)**

Then Paul answered, "Why are you weeping and breaking my heart? I am ready not only to be bound, but also to die in Jerusalem for the name of the Lord Jesus."

**(Acts 21:13 NIV)**

Not only so, but we also glory in our sufferings, because we know that suffering produces perseverance; perseverance, character; and character, hope.

**(Romans 5:3–4 NIV)**

*Count it all joy, my brothers, when you meet trials of various kinds, for you know that the testing of your faith produces steadfastness. And let steadfastness have its full effect, that you may be perfect and complete, lacking in nothing.*

**(James 1:2–4 ESV)**

*My dear friends, do not be surprised at the painful test you are suffering, as though something unusual were happening to you. Rather be glad that you are sharing Christ's sufferings, so that you may be full of joy when his glory is revealed.*

**(1 Peter 4:12–13 GNT)**

# TAKE INVENTORY

As we look back to the beginning of our caregiving journey and compare it to our present, it is helpful to take a mental inventory. Questions to ponder include: Are we more compassionate? Have we been faithful in the little things? Have we learned to trust Him more? Are we able to see others the way Jesus might see them more so now than at the beginning of this caregiving expedition? Are we able to have grace for ourselves? What do we still need to lay down at the throne? Hopefully, we are able to see some steps toward the goal and be encouraged by our inventory. Sometimes when the changes are so gradual and small, we do not recognize them. But every time we submit our lives to the Lord and we are willing to take up His cross, it is a win.

Dear Lord, help us to see the progress we have made in our caregiving season. You measure things so differently than we do. You just want our hearts fully devoted to You, and then the rest will be a natural part of the process. We want to embrace all that you have for our loved ones and for us. We are so thankful that You give us beauty for ashes and that You multiply blessings. Thank You for faithfully walking with us and for teaching us and molding us along the way. Amen.

*Then Jesus said to his disciples, "If anyone wants to come with me, he must forget self, carry his cross, and follow me. For whoever wants to save his own life will lose it; but whoever loses his life for my sake will find it.*

(Matthew 16:24–25 GNT)

*Not that I have already obtained this or am already perfect, but I press on to make it my own, because Jesus Christ has made me his own. Brothers, I do not consider that I have made it my own. But one thing I do: forgetting what lies behind and straining forward to what lies ahead, I press on toward the goal for the prize of the upward call of God in Christ Jesus.*

**(Philippians 3:12–14 ESV)**

*But the Spirit produces love, joy, peace, patience, kindness, goodness, faithfulness, humility, and self-control. There is no law against such things as these.*

**(Galatians 5:22–23 GNT)**

*"Father, if you are willing, take this cup from me; yet not my will, but yours be done."*

**(Luke 22:42 NIV)**

*Yet, O LORD, You are our Father; We are the clay, and You our Potter, And we all are the work of Your hand.*

**(Isaiah 64:8 AMP)**

*But first and most importantly seek (aid at, strive after) His kingdom and His righteousness [His way of doing and being right—the attitude and character of God], and all these things will be given to you also.*

**(Matthew 6:33 AMP)**

*"Do not store up riches for yourselves here on earth, where moths and rust destroy, and robbers break in and steal. Instead, store up riches for yourselves in heaven, where moths and rust cannot destroy, and robbers cannot break in and steal. For your heart will always be where your riches are."*

**(Matthew 6:19–21 GNT)**

*and provide for those who grieve in Zion—to bestow on them a crown of beauty instead of ashes, the oil of joy instead of mourning, and a garment of praise instead of a spirit of despair. They will be called oaks of righteousness, a planting of the LORD for the display of his splendor.*

**(Isaiah 61:3 NIV)**

# LOVE

After a long week, with my energy gone, I sat down to seek my Father. "Lord," I asked, "What is going on here?" I sensed His presence answer me with a question. "Have you learned to love yet?" I was stunned. The question hit me between the eyes. I thought back over the last many years of caregiving. I was reminded of all the ways I had failed or fallen short, and I felt remorse. But quickly, He swept my memory full of times I sacrificed my time, myself, my heart to serve. I focused back on the Lord, and I replied, "I'm learning, Lord. I'm in the process. Teach me. I want to love well."

Dear Lord, we do want to learn to love as You did. Help us to grow in our love for You and for others. Thank you for faithfully being with us every step of the way. We realize that we cannot see the full view of our lives the way You can, so we trust Your ways. May we have the mind of Christ. May we exhibit the love of the Father. May we walk this journey equipped with the compassion and counsel from the Holy Spirit. May we honor You in this caregiving journey. In Jesus Name, we pray these things. Amen.

*Whoever finds his life [in this world] will [eventually] lose it [through death], and whoever loses his life [in this world] for my sake will find it [that is, life with Me for all eternity].*

**(Matthew 10:23 AMP)**

*My command is this: Love each other as I have loved you. Greater love has no one than this: that he lay down his life for his friends.*

**(John 15:12–13 NIV)**

*A new command I give you: Love one another. As I have loved you, so you must love one another.*

**(John 13:34 NIV)**

*We know what real love is because Jesus gave up his life for us. So we also ought to give up our lives for our brothers and sisters.*

**(1 John 3:16 NLT)**

*I have been crucified with Christ. It is no longer I who live, but Christ who lives in me. And the life I now live in the flesh I live by faith in the Son of God, who loved me and gave himself for me.*

**(Galatians 2:20 ESV)**

*Love is patient and kind; love does not envy or boast; it is not arrogant or rude. It does not insist on its own way; it is not irritable or resentful; it does not rejoice at wrongdo-*

*ing, but rejoices with the truth. Love bears all things, believes all things, hopes all things, endures all things. Love never ends.*

**(1 Corinthians 13:4–8a ESV)**

# EPILOGUE

If you are finishing this devotional, I assume you are wondering what the end of my story looks like. At this time, I am still on my caregiving journey. My mom lives with me and is a cheerful yet often confused lover of Jesus. We have learned to laugh more and to cry frequently together.

My dad lives in an assisted living facility, and my brothers and I are beginning arrangements to put him on hospice service. Dad still breaks a big smile when I enter his room, even though he could not tell you how I am related to him or, depending on the day, my name.

Each day seems to bring new dilemmas, but I can look back and see that my God has carried me before, and I can trust Him for the future. I can also see that some rough edges of selfishness have been carved off of my life, and I am a better person for having walked this valley. I am still in the process of learning to love.

My hope for you is that you gathered some encouragement and peace from these readings. My prayer is that you will know there are many others out there who can understand your situation. You are never alone. Others are nearby, but most importantly, our amazing God is always with you.

Peace to you as we continue to live the gospel.

# REFERENCES

*Life Application Study Bible: New International Version [NIV]*. 2012. Wheaton, Ill: Tyndale House Publishers, Inc.

Petterson, Eugene H. 2005. *The Message [MSG]*. Tyndale House Publishers, Inc. https://www.biblegateway.com/versions/Message-MSG-Bible/#booklist.

*The Holy Bible: American Standard Version [ASV]*. 1901. Thomas Nelson and Sons. Public domain. https://www.biblegateway.com/versions/American-Standard-Version-ASV-Bible/#booklist.

*The Holy Bible: Amplified Bible [AMP]*. 2015. La Habra, California: The Lockman Foundation. https://www.biblegateway.com/versions/Amplified-Bible-AMP/#booklist.

*The Holy Bible: Berean Study Bible [BSB]*. 2016. 1st editio. https://biblehub.com/bsb/genesis/1.htm.

*The Holy Bible: English Standard Version [ESV]*. 2007. Wheaton, Ill: Crossway Bibles. Public domain. https://www.biblegateway.com/versions/English-Standard-Version-ESV-Bible/#booklist.

*The Holy Bible: New American Standard Bible [NASB]*. 2015. The Lockman Foundation. http://www.lockman.org/nasb/index.php.

*The Holy Bible: New American Standard Bible [NASB1995]*. 1995. The Lockman Foundation. http://www.lockman.org/nasb/index.php.

*The Holy Bible: New Living Translation [NLT]*. 2013.

Carol Stream: Tyndale House Foundation. Tyndale House Publishers, Inc. https://www.biblegateway.com/versions/New-Living-Translation-NLT-Bible/#booklist.

*The Holy Bible: The Passion Translation [TPT]*. 2020. BroadStreet Publishing Group, LLC.

# ABOUT THE AUTHOR

Kay Tuel is a retired family therapist, chaplain, university lecturer, and an ordained minister. Presently she leads seminars for nurses, medical staff, college students, and others regarding how to cope with death and dying and how to live life fully to the finish. She has produced some educational films on end-of-life issues such as grief, loss, and living with Alzheimer's.

Most of her passion for sharing comes from over eighteen years of caring for her father, who survived a cerebral infarction. His stroke left him with the inability to communicate and difficulties in walking. In the past eight years, she has had more caregiving experiences from having her mother live with her after suffering a head trauma.

These life situations have provided her with better insight into the needs of those who are infirm or otherwise unable to care for themselves. Caregiving can be a tough and unrecognized role. It is her hope that her experiences can benefit those in similar situations.